FAITHFUL
Celebrations

MAKING TIME FOR GOD
FROM ADVENT THROUGH EPIPHANY

Edited by

SHARON ELY PEARSON

CHURCH
PUBLISHING
INCORPORATED

Scripture texts referred to in this work are taken from the *New Revised Standard Version Bible*, copyright © 1989 by the Division of Christian Education of the National Council of Churches of Christ in the USA, and are used by permission.

Acknowledgments: Faithful Celebrations is the work of many unnamed contributors, as well as Carolyn Chilton, Janie Stevens, Dina Strong, Sylvia DeVillers, Sara Fontana, Kathy Finely, Rita Mailander, Kathy Coffey, Dirk deVries, Sharon Ely Pearson, and Jim Wahler.

Illustrators: Sally Brewer Lawrence, Anne Kosel, Victoria Bergesen, Tom Lybeck, and Paula Becker

Church Publishing
19 East 34th Street
New York, NY 10016
www.churchpublishing.org

Cover design by Jennifer Kopec, 2Pug Design
Typeset by Rose Design

Library of Congress Cataloging-in-Publication Data

Names: Pearson, Sharon Ely, editor.
Title: Faithful celebrations : making time for God from Advent through
  Epiphany / edited by Sharon Ely Pearson.
Description: New York : Church Publishing, 2018.
Identifiers: LCCN 2017055408 (print) | LCCN 2018016575 (ebook) | ISBN
  9780898690484 (ebook) | ISBN 9780898690477 (pbk.)
Subjects: LCSH: Church year. | Communities—Religious aspects—Christianity.
  | Fellowship.
Classification: LCC BV30 (ebook) | LCC BV30 .F349 2018 (print) | DDC
  263/.9—dc23
LC record available at https://lccn.loc.gov/2017055408

Printed in the United States of America

Contents

Introduction

But speaking the truth in love, we must grow up in every way into him who is the head, into Christ, from whom the whole body, joined and knit together by every ligament with which it is equipped, as each part is working properly, promotes the body's growth in building itself up in love.

—Ephesians 4:15–16

I n a small way, this book's intention is to help the Body of Christ grow in understanding and "build itself up through love" at church or home. Celebrations, gatherings, and rituals help members of every generation find both individual meaning and common ground, all through the medium of direct experience, no matter the age of the participant. *Faithful Celebrations: Making Time for God from Advent through Epiphany* offers a multitude of ideas for planning an event focused on a season or day of the calendar year that will bring families together and build strong communities of faith, whether it is in the home or a congregational setting.

Through such occasions we can become better acquainted with our extended family—young and old together—in any setting. We can take steps toward making our congregation (or neighborhood) the warm, nurturing community we long for in our fragmented world. Older adults sometimes feel a sense of displacement in congregational life today, and younger people are increasingly looking to a variety of sources for spiritual nurture and faith practice.

Singing, praying, eating, and creating memories together enhances our wellbeing and makes our connections to one another stronger. Undergirding our experiences is the presence of God among us, nurturing us and working through us to help us grow in the knowledge and love of Christ Jesus.

Through community celebrations, we can experience scripture and traditions in a fresh way that can give beauty and meaning to our daily lives. Within these pages you will find ideas to hold a theme-based event, or simply ideas to supplement other activities you have planned. This abundance allows you to choose only those activities that meet your congregation's or family's particular needs—and fit your timeframe. *Faithful Celebrations* will help you and your family—at home, school, or church—learn more and experience these particular Christian seasons:

- Advent
- The Annunciation (This is recognized on March 25 of the Christian calendar, but it is so connected to the story of the birth of Jesus it makes sense to celebrate it with children during the Advent season.)
- Our Lady of Guadalupe
- Las Posadas
- Christmas
- Epiphany

ALL AGES GROWING TOGETHER

Many of the formative experiences in life happen when several generations are together. In our society we tend to separate people by ages mainly for education and employment. In recent years, Christian formation programs have made this same separation of generations, but more and more religious educators are recommending programs in which adults and children learn together. It is a way to pass on faith—generation to generation. Old learn from young, and young learn from old.

Faithful Celebrations is designed to meet the need for generations to learn together. This approach requires that we venture beyond traditional learning methods into the world of experiential learning. Just as old and young alike can participate in vacations, trips, holidays, and family events together, learning more about our relationship with God can take place with all generations growing together. This may mean that adults work alongside children, helping them as well as listening to them as full partners in an activity or discussion. It means allowing children to experience things for themselves, not doing things for them but with them.

WHEN, WHERE, WHY, AND HOW

Finding time and resources to add another component to already full schedules, both in families and in congregations, can be a challenge. Within your community of faith, look to different groups who could successfully host an intergenerational gathering. One promising lead might be to invite your youth organization to be in charge of leading one or more sessions. Consider also the possibility of asking different congregational organizations to host a given session. In a typical community of faith, consider using these ideas as:

- intergenerational and multi-age programming
- seasonal church gatherings for families
- primary Christian education material for a small church
- supplementary material for large Christian education programs
- supplementary material for classes in church-based schools
- home study Christian education programs
- small-community or base-community Christian education
- supplementary material for family sacramental programs

In a home setting, families can use these activities for:

- family vacations and holidays
- neighborhood or community events

- home schooling and education
- gatherings of friends and families

Each chapter in *Faithful Celebrations* begins with an Introduction that includes background material and key ideas for each Celebration. Use this content to inspire your vision of what the event needs to be, for you, your planning committee, and your congregation or family. The pages that follow are organized by type of activity, such as opening prayer, story, craft, food, drama, music, game, or more. It will always conclude with a closing activity of prayer.

Each activity or experience will include a very brief explanation for the leader, followed by a list of materials needed and step-by-step directions. The materials called for in this book are simple and inexpensive. Those common to most activities are:

- Bibles
- whiteboard, poster board, or newsprint pad with markers
- felt pens
- crayons (regular and oversized for young children)
- drawing paper
- glue
- scissors

From time to time links will be offered to supplemental online materials; there are also downloadable resources of craft patterns and templates available for free at *www.churchpublishing.org/faithful celebrations3*.

Almighty God, you have poured upon us the new light of your incarnate Word: Grant that this light, enkindled in our hearts, may shine forth in our lives from generation to generation; through Jesus Christ our Lord, who lives and reigns with you, in the unity of the Holy Spirit, one God, for ever and ever. *Amen.*

—*Collect for the First Sunday after Christmas Day* (adapted),
Book of Common Prayer, p. 213

Chapter 1

ADVENT

INTRODUCTION

Advent, the first season of the Church year, begins on the fourth Sunday before Christmas. (This is the Sunday falling on or nearest November 30.) Varying from twenty-two to twenty-eight days, the season ends on Christmas Eve. The liturgical colors for Advent are purple and blue.

We spend this time preparing for the celebration of Christmas. We make gifts and buy them. We cover the presents in wrappings plain and fancy, making each gift as secret as the child who grew in Mary's womb. We prepare and receive cards, wishing each friend and loved one a happy and holy celebration of Christmas. Our houses are perhaps more fragrant now than at any other time of year, with a heady mix of the aromas of candle wax, evergreens, and spices.

Even those who don't go to church are certain that the coming Christmas is a time of great joy. Along with the canned carols at the malls and plastic Santas on the lawns, we need to understand the longing for joy that prompts them. We need to find ways to enrich our own and our community's preparations with the deeper meanings of Advent.

Advent Means Coming

We need to remember, for example, that the word *advent* means "coming." During Advent, we prepare for the celebration of the coming of Jesus as a babe in Bethlehem.

That birth fulfilled both the words of Israel's prophets and the events in Israel's history that each speak of God's saving grace. Thus, the Church has appointed scriptures for Advent that tell of God's promises to the people of Israel, especially prophecies that suggest the coming of a Messiah and a messianic age.

"You are God's beloved," Abraham heard in an alien land, and "God will be yours," promised Isaiah. Every covenant and prophecy—from the exodus to the foretelling of the nations' return to Jerusalem—recalled the promise of union with God. In Jesus, the promise is fulfilled.

A Season of Paradox

But Advent is also a season of paradox. We have inherited this two-fold emphasis on joyful expectation and as well as somber repentance from the early Church. In the fourth century, Christians began celebrating Christmas as a religious festival, replacing the older pagan feast of the Unconquered Sun. It follows that in part of Christendom, the Church sought to make Advent a period of joy, glowing with the power of the Son of God.

In other places, the Church directed candidates who would be received into the Church on Epiphany, January 6, to fast during the preceding midwinter weeks. For this reason, Advent eventually became a time of penitent preparation for all Christians.

Preparing the Way for the New Creation

During Advent, we also recall and honor those who prepared the way for Jesus, and especially those who welcomed his birth: Zechariah, Elizabeth, Mary, Joseph, and others. We hear the stories of preparation. We sing carols of expectation.

But our expectation is not limited to the past events of Bethlehem. Jesus is coming, not only once to Bethlehem over two thousand years ago, but also today in word and sacrament. Jesus is coming again, in great glory, at the end of all time. Thus, in Advent, we also read scriptures that tell of an ultimate judgment, the end of this age, and a new reign of the kingdom of God.

These scriptures suggest questions: Might Jesus' second coming encompass both an outward, physical event and an inner event of the mind and heart? Indeed, it is often the apocalyptic events of our lives that bring us from a time of "running our own shows" (at great distance from God) into a new, deeper relationship with God.

So now we watch and wait. We watch and wait as the days of Advent run to Christmas. We watch and wait as the Church prepares place and song and heart for our infant Savior. We watch and wait for he who comes to us, in scripture and in Eucharist, who feeds us with his life. We watch and wait for the one who comes to fulfill all things, to make the whole creation new.

We watch and wait for Jesus, and he is coming.

Beyond the Celebration

The Advent season lends itself particularly well to giving to others. Beyond the Giving Tree activity, invite participants to take advantage of the many opportunities offered by most congregations to assist those in need through food collections, financial donations, wrapping and distributing gifts, etc. Invite persons from church or local social service organizations to speak to the group, emphasizing the ongoing needs of the poor. You might organize specific outreach opportunities throughout Advent and provide sign-up sheets during your Advent celebration.

WORSHIP

Opening Prayer

Begin the celebration by praying (or singing together) an Advent hymn:

Come, Thou Long Expected Jesus

Come, thou long expected Jesus, born to set thy people free;
from our fears and sins release us, let us find our rest in thee.

Israel's strength and consolation, hope of all the earth thou art:
dear desire of every nation, joy of every longing heart.

Born thy people to deliver, born a child, and yet a king,
born to reign in us for ever, now thy gracious kingdom bring.

By thine own eternal Spirit rule in all our hearts along;
by thine all sufficient merit raise us to thy glorious throne.

CRAFTS

Advent Wreaths

The Advent wreath is a tradition that helps us take time out from our busy Christmas preparations to open our hearts to Jesus.

The circular form of the wreath, like God's love, is never-ending. The greenery that covers it reminds us of everlasting life and hope because evergreen trees are green even in the midst of winter.

The candles are symbols of the light God brings us. Three of them are dark "royal" purple or Sarum blue (from the medieval Sarum rite in England). Both symbolize preparation, penitence, and royalty to welcome the new King. The purple of Advent is also the color of suffering used during Lent and Holy Week. This points to an important connection between Jesus' birth and death. Deep blue is the color of the clear, predawn sky, the color that covers the earth in the hours before the sun rises in the east. Most of us are not looking at the sky at that hour—perhaps we're still asleep, or too weary to notice it as we get ready for work or school. Nonetheless, a deep, dark blue is the color that covers us in the dark, cold hours before the sun dawns. Thus, the deep blue for Advent reminds us of the season of expectation and anticipation of the dawn of Christ.

The fourth candle is pink and is lit on the Third Sunday of Advent when we celebrate with special joy. Some people light a white candle, the Christ candle, in the center of the wreath on Christmas Day.

Make an Advent wreath to symbolize the everlasting nature of God's love and light. If you are doing this as a church-wide event, offer several methods by setting up materials for each method at separate tables, and invite families to work together to make an Advent wreath of their choice for their homes. Provide families with additional materials that they can use for their own family Advent wreath observances.

Wreath 1

Materials

- florist's wire, heavy and lightweight
- evergreens
- short candle holders, 4 (or 5) for each wreath
- candles: 3 purple (or blue) and 1 rose (or pink) for each wreath
- *optional:* florist's or modeling clay; purple ribbon; sprays of berries; pine cones; white candle

Directions

1. Bend the heavy wire into a 12" diameter circle. (To make the wreath sturdier and fuller, you might choose to make a second, smaller circle, place it within the first, and wire the two together with short lengths of wire.)
2. Trim the circular form with evergreens, bound to it with lightweight wire. You may wish to put the wreath on a plate or tray with a rim, in order to keep the wreath fresh with water in the container for moisture.
3. Put four short candle holders at equal distance around the circle. Save the white candle and holder to place in the center on Christmas.
4. If necessary, use bits of modeling or florist's clay to hold the candles securely in the candle holders.
5. Add a purple (or blue) bow, berries, or pinecones, if desired, for decoration.

Wreath 2

Materials

- dinner plate for each wreath (ask each family to bring a plate from home)
- florist's clay
- candles: 3 purple (or blue) and 1 rose (or pink) for each wreath

- lightweight florist's wire
- evergreens
- *optional:* 1 white candle for each wreath; purple ribbon; sprays of berries; pinecones

Directions

1. Use florist's clay to secure the three purple and one pink candles to the dinner plate. (Add one white candle in the center to represent Christ, if desired.)
2. Use lightweight florist's wire to bind small bundles of greenery and place these on the plate to form the wreath. Add a purple (or blue) bow, berries, or pinecones to decorate the wreath, if desired.

Wreath 3

Materials

- 1–1½" thick cross sections of a log 10–12" in diameter
- drill with ½" bit
- candles: 3 purple (or blue) and 1 rose (or pink) for each wreath
- staple gun and staples
- evergreens

Directions

1. Drill four or five ½" deep holes in each cross section of log.
2. Place one candle in each hole.
3. Use the staple gun to attach evergreens to the wood.

Jesse Tree Booklets and Ornaments

Jesse was the father of King David, and both were ancestors of Jesus. Many years after Jesse lived, the prophet Isaiah told of a new tree that would sprout from the family tree of Jesse—a new king would arise from among David's descendants.

"A shoot shall come out from the stump of Jesse, and a branch shall grow out of his roots."—Isaiah 11:1

A Jesse Tree can be an evergreen tree, a fabric wall hanging in the shape of a tree, or a bare branch anchored in a pot of rocks. The custom is to add a decoration to the tree each day during Advent. The decorations are symbols of Jesse and other men and women of the Old Testament who prepared the way for Jesus.

This activity includes directions for making Jesse Tree decorations and a booklet to use at home along with the decorations. Alternately, you could make decorations to use on a Jesse Tree for your church.

Jesse Tree Booklets

Prior to beginning the activity, briefly explain the custom of the Jesse Tree, inviting each person to make a Jesse Tree book to take home. Plan to demonstrate as you give directions.

Materials

- white 8½" x 11" paper, 7 sheets per person
- 8½" x 11" purple construction paper, 1 sheet per person
- pink yarn or satin ribbon
- hole punch
- scissors
- rubber cement or glue stick

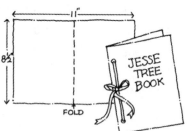

- copies of Jesse Tree symbols (page 9), 1 set per person (download at *www.churchpublishing.org/faithfulcelebrations3*)
- markers or crayons

Directions

1. To make the book, fold seven white sheets of paper in half. Tuck each sheet inside another. (The size of the book will be 8½" x 5½" wide.)

2. Fold a sheet of construction paper in like fashion and put this around the pages as a cover. Punch two holes near the spine of the booklet. Run a piece of yarn through the holes and tie the booklet together.

3. Number the pages 1–28. Take the Jesse Tree symbols and cut along the solid lines so that you have a slip of paper for each day of Advent. Glue a slip to each page, in consecutive order from 1 to 28. Use crayons or markers to decorate illustrations.

Note: The actual number of days in Advent can vary depending upon which day of the week Christmas falls. In essence, you'll have enough pages in each booklet to observe four full weeks of "Advent" prior to Christmas Day, even if the actual number of days in Advent is less than twenty-eight.

Jesse Tree Ornaments

Invite participants to make a set of Jesse Tree ornaments to use at home or church on a bare branch tree, felt tree, or evergreen. Provide copies of symbols, but also invite participants to create their own symbols, if they wish.

Materials

- copies of Jesse Tree symbols (on the right) (download at *www.churchpublishing.org /faithfulcelebrations3*)

Full-size patterns can be downloaded *at www.churchpublishing .org/faithfulcelebrations3*

- felt, in assorted colors
- scissors
- glue
- ribbon
- *optional:* sequins, glitter, pom-poms

Directions

1. Suggest a collage technique for constructing the ornaments. For example: The crown for David could be cut from yellow felt, then decorated with glued-on scraps of felt in bright colors or with sequins or glitter.

2. Add a ribbon loop with glue to the top of the ornament for hanging.

Mural of the New Creation

Invite everyone to work together to make a mural that illustrates Jesus' bringing the new creation.

Isaiah 65:17–25

For I am about to create new heavens
    and a new earth;
the former things shall not be remembered
    or come to mind.
But be glad and rejoice for ever
    in what I am creating;
for I am about to create Jerusalem as a joy,
    and its people as a delight.
I will rejoice in Jerusalem,
    and delight in my people;
no more shall the sound of weeping be heard in it,
    or the cry of distress.
No more shall there be in it
    an infant that lives but a few days,
    or an old person who does not live out a lifetime;

for one who dies at a hundred years will be considered a youth,
   and one who falls short of a hundred will be considered accursed.
They shall build houses and inhabit them;
   they shall plant vineyards and eat their fruit.
They shall not build and another inhabit;
   they shall not plant and another eat;
for like the days of a tree shall the days of my people be,
   and my chosen shall long enjoy the work of their hands.
They shall not labor in vain,
   or bear children for calamity;
for they shall be offspring blessed by the LORD—
   and their descendants as well.
Before they call I will answer,
   while they are yet speaking I will hear.
The wolf and the lamb shall feed together,
   the lion shall eat straw like the ox;
   but the serpent—its food shall be dust!
They shall not hurt or destroy
   on all my holy mountain,
says the LORD.

Materials

- Bibles
- butcher paper, approximate 10 feet in length
- crayons or markers
- whiteboard, poster board, or newsprint
- masking tape

Directions

1. Read Isaiah 65:17–25 to the participants, inviting everyone to read along silently. Ask the following questions:

   - Why do we read about God's new creation in Advent?
   - What will we find in the new creation?
   - How would you feel living there?

2. List answers on whiteboard, newsprint, or poster board for all to see. Mention, if no one else has, that Jesus brings the new creation to God's people.

3. Using the ideas generated by the group, use markers or crayons to create the scene on a long sheet of butcher paper that you have taped to the wall. (Make sure that it is within reach of the youngest participants and that markers will not bleed through the paper.)

Simple Christmas Ornaments

Even the smallest child can participant in this activity with assistance.

Materials
- small, gold metallic paper doilies
- glue
- old Christmas cards
- thread or string (gold, if possible)
- scissors

Directions
1. Make a simple Christmas tree ornament by gluing two gold metallic doilies together, shiny sides out.

2. Cut a small nativity story figure or other design out of an old Christmas card and glue the figure in the center of one of the doilies.

3. String gold thread through the top of the ornament as a hanger. (One of these could be tucked in with a Christmas card to a friend.)

Gift Wrap

For many, Christmas is all about gift-giving. While the project is underway, this activity gives an opportunity to talk about why this custom came to be at Christmas, with the ultimate gift God gave to us: Jesus.

Materials

- butcher paper or shelf paper
- pages from the classified section of a newspaper
- objects for printing: cookie cutters, empty spools, jar lids, corks, square rubber erasers, sponges cut into the shapes of stars, trees, and angels
- thick red and green tempera paint
- cookie sheets or disposable pie pans
- paper towels
- portable laundry drying racks or clothesline (with clothespins)
- plastic tablecloths as drop cloths under the drying racks or clothesline as well as on the tables to protect the surface from unwanted paint

Directions

1. Make a stamp pad for printing by putting ten or so paper towels on a cookie sheet or in a pie pan and saturating the paper towels with thick red or green paint. Make enough stamp pads to scatter around the tables where the activity will take place.
2. Give each participant a 3-foot length of paper or a page of newspaper.
3. Invite everyone to make wrapping paper by dipping various objects into paint and pressing the objects onto the paper. Repeated designs are especially effective.
4. Drape or hang them on the racks or clothesline to dry.

STORYTELLING AND BIBLE STUDY

Christmas Memories

This activity involves choosing a favorite Christmas memory and writing a story about it. It then goes a step further by engaging everyone to contemplate what makes a recollection so special and unforgettable.

Materials

- paper
- pens or pencils

Directions

1. Ask each participant to make a list of special Christmas memories, choose one of their favorites, and write its story with as many details as possible. Allow 10–15 minutes.

2. Next ask each participant to list all the elements that made that memory special. Suggested elements might include:

   - food
   - presents
   - one special gift
   - family
   - friends
   - music
   - prayer
   - house decorations
   - weather
   - place
   - church service

3. Ask participants to circle the three most important elements on the list. Allow 10 minutes for this activity.

4. Divide the group into small groups of 4–5 members each to discuss these questions:

   - What are the most important elements of our favorite Christmas memories?
   - What elements of our Christmas observances do we spend the most time or money on today?
   - What do we want more of in our observances? What do we want less of in our observances?
   - How can we make these changes?

Paper Advent Banners

The word "advent" means "coming" and this activity will help every-one learn who is coming and when.

Advance preparation

Before the session, print out the questions and scripture references on p. 16 and cut into separate slips for each group (or download at *www.churchpublishing.org/faithfulcelebrations3*).

Materials

- Bibles
- slips of paper printed with questions and scripture references
- scissors
- 6' sheets of white butcher paper, 1 per group
- large sheets of tissue paper in various colors
- rubber cement
- empty margarine tubs (to hold rubber cement)
- small house-painting brushes
- black markers

Directions

1. Have participants count off in order to divide into random groups of six to ten people each, making sure that each group includes both children and adults.
2. Furnish each group with at least one Bible, craft materials, and one of the questions.
3. Instruct groups to read their question aloud. Look up answers in Bibles, adults helping children as needed. Answer the question and decide how the group will quickly make a paper banner to illustrate the answer. (Tearing the tissue paper into large shapes will work more easily than cutting out many small shapes.)
4. On each banner write the word *Advent* and write phrases from scripture that answer the question.

5. After everyone has finished, reassemble and ask someone from each group to read the group's question and explain how its banner answers the questions.

Tip: As you give instructions for an activity, jot key words on newsprint, whiteboard, or poster board for everyone to refer to as they work. Key words for this activity might include: read and answer question, illustrate answer, write Advent and scripture phrases on the banner.

Banner Questions

Group 1: When and how did Jesus come to us in the very first Advent?
Matthew 1:18–25; Luke 1:26–38; John 1:1–5, 14

Group 2: When and how will Jesus come to us in the future at what we call his second coming?
Matthew 25:1–13; Mark 13:24–27; Luke 21:25–28; 1 Corinthians 15:20–28

Group 3: How does Jesus come to us here and now in the Eucharist?
Matthew 26:26–29; Mark 14:22–25; Luke 22:14–20; John 6:32–40; 1 Corinthians 11:23–26

An Advent Newspaper

What if you were there at the time of Jesus' birth? What if you were asked to write a first-person account for a newspaper, blog, magazine, or news program about the event? What if this was an event that happened in our world today? This activity invites small groups or individuals to create a newspaper to share this good news with the world. Their newspaper can contain a variety of "columns" like today's newspapers, including illustrations and photos. This activity could be adapted to produce videos instead of newspapers. Some suggestions: editorials, cartoons, interviews, opinion polls, drawings.

Materials

- Bibles
- paper

- pens or pencils
- felt pens
- crayons
- 18" x 24" newsprint paper
- tape

Directions

1. Divide everyone into three groups of mixed ages (if possible). Ask each group to make a newspaper about the good news of Jesus' coming.

2. Ask the *first* group to make a newspaper about the coming of Jesus as a baby to Bethlehem. Refer the group to Luke 2:1–20.

3. Ask the *second* group to make a newspaper about the coming of Jesus to us today in word and sacrament. Suggest interviewing each other about experiences with Jesus in word and sacrament. For example, the participants might ask each other:

   - What makes you feel close to Jesus?
   - What are your favorite stories of Jesus and why?
   - What does the bread mean to you? What does the wine mean to you?

4. Ask the *third* group to make a newspaper about the coming of Jesus at the end of time. Suggest the use of the prophecies in Isaiah 25:6–9, Matthew 25:31–45, and Revelation 21:1–4 as resources.

5. When each piece is written, each group can mount its finished items on a sheet of newsprint as though laying out a newspaper page. Tape the finished newspapers to a wall for all to read.

An additional resource

Heather Annis's book *The Book of Comic Prayer: Using Art and Humor to Transform Youth Ministry* (Morehouse, 2016) offers ways to engage youth in the creation of comic strips for sharing the Good News.

MARKING TIME
Weekly Advent Calendars

Make Advent calendars individually or in groups of three or four members each. This calendar will feature envelopes for each day of the week, Sunday through Saturday, in which a daily idea or activity will be hidden. When a new week begins, new ideas are added to each envelope to begin the process again, each week leading up to Christmas.

Make enough calendars so that each person will receive one. Put all the calendars from all the groups together, and ask one or two children to distribute one to each person.

Materials
- newsprint
- glue
- envelopes (8 per calendar)
- burlap or poster board (any color) or green poster board (1 per calendar)
- scissors
- pens or pencils
- 3" x 5" memo pads or blank index cards
- *optional:* Christmas gift wrap; clear tape

Directions
1. Together, brainstorm activities appropriate for Advent, noting them on newsprint, such as:
   - Add a figure to your crèche.
   - Make a Christmas card for a friend.
   - Read Mary's song in Luke 1:46–55.
   - Give coins to a Salvation Army kettle.
   - Sing an Advent song.
   - Make a present for Jesus.

2. Ask each group or individual to glue eight envelopes down the length of a strip of burlap or poster board. If desired, first cover one side of the poster board with Christmas gift wrap, folding it over the edges of the poster board, and taping the gift wrap in place. Or use green poster board and cut it in the shape of a large Christmas tree, making sure that all eight envelopes will fit on it.

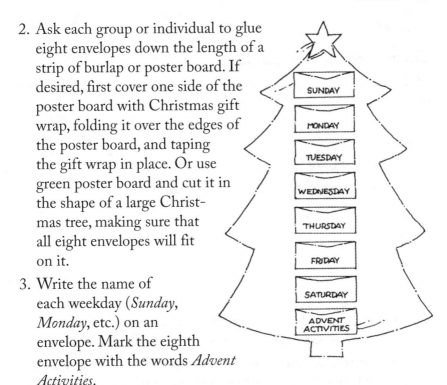

3. Write the name of each weekday (*Sunday, Monday*, etc.) on an envelope. Mark the eighth envelope with the words *Advent Activities*.

4. Have the participants write the activities on slips of memo paper, one slip for each activity, providing one activity for each day of Advent. Put all the slips in the envelope marked Advent Activities.

Invite everyone to post Advent calendars on a wall at home. Each Sunday during Advent, take seven slips of paper from the Advent Activities envelope on your calendar and put one slip in each of the other envelopes. Each day pull a slip out of the appropriate envelope and follow its instructions.

DRAMA

Christmas Card Puppets

Make a set of stick puppets to use in dramatizing the Christmas story.

Materials

- assortment of old Christmas cards
- tongue depressors or strips of cardboard
- glue
- scissors
- Bible

Directions

1. Cut out nativity figures from old Christmas cards, and glue the figures to tongue depressors or strips of cardboard.
2. Each person can use their finished figures to act out the story you read from Luke 2:1–20—or they can tell the story in their own words as they act it out.

GAMES

Advent Word Search

Search for the people who played a part in the story of Jesus' birth.

Materials

- copies of the puzzle below (download at *www.churchpublishing.org/faithfulcelebrations3*)
- pens or pencils
- Bibles

Directions

1. To include all ages for this activity, form small groups. Adults can then help young children find the answers.
2. Circle the 10 names that are hidden in a vertical or horizontal line in the puzzle below (Anna, Elizabeth, Gabriel, Jesus, John, Joseph, Mary, Shepherds, Simeon, Zechariah).
3. Talk about what part each person played in the Nativity story. If you need help, you can find their stories in Luke 1:26–45, 57–66, and 2:4–15, 21–38.

S	I	M	A	R	J	E	S	U	S
H	Z	E	C	H	A	R	I	A	H
I	E	L	I	Z	O	N	M	N	E
G	H	I	M	O	J	S	E	S	P
A	O	Z	M	C	O	U	O	G	H
B	Q	A	A	K	S	X	N	A	E
R	A	B	R	I	E	L	O	N	R
I	N	E	Y	M	P	A	N	G	D
E	N	T	J	O	H	N	E	E	S
L	A	H	N	N	D	S	G	L	A

PRAYER ACTIVITIES

Quiet Time, Festive Time

This is not so much a single activity as a plan for an evening for adults and older children, combining the penitence and joy of Advent. The first part of the evening is silent, except for music. Ideally a large, open room with a rug works best, so that people are comfortable sitting on the floor.

Communicate in advance to participants that the first part of the evening will be a time for reflection and the second part will be a party. Ask everyone to bring food and drink to share at the party. (You might want to plan some separate activities for young children during the quiet time and invite them in to join the party later.)

Materials

- evergreen boughs
- 5–6 candles in holders
- recorded Christmas music or musicians from your worship community
- prepared slips of paper with names of figures in the Nativity story (*Mary, Joseph, shepherd, donkey, sheep,* etc.)
- basket or container to hold slips of paper
- 5–6 pictures of situations or places in our world where there is poverty, violence, or other tragedy
- craft supplies (paper and fabric scraps, cardboard tubes, pipe cleaners, aluminum foil, modeling clay, cotton balls, glue, scissors, etc.)
- small natural objects (pinecones, twigs, rocks, etc.)
- refreshments brought by participants

Advance preparation

Since the latter part of this activity is a festive time of drinking and eating together, you will need—in advance—to ask participants to bring a variety of snacks and beverages to share.

Directions

1. Before participants arrive, set up five or six places around the room where people will pray. At each of these, have a lighted candle on the floor. Encircle the candle with evergreen boughs and a picture that shows people or situations that need God's healing love.

2. Set the craft supplies, including the small natural objects, on a table.

3. Post signs asking everyone to enter silently. Maintain this silence until everyone has gathered.

4. When everyone has arrived, explain that you will pass a basket with slips of paper. On each slip is written the name of one of the figures in the Nativity story. Ask each person to select a slip, choose craft supplies, and find a corner in which to create a figure representing the name on the slip.

5. Maintain silence while everyone works. Encourage each participant to think about why this particular figure happened to be the one he or she received. Or to put it another way, "Why did this figure choose you?"

6. After participants have made their figures, invite them to visit the prayer stations around the room, placing their figures at each candle as they meditate briefly on the image at each station. Encourage them to reflect and ask God what needs to be born inside themselves this Christmas.

7. After they have stopped at every station, have them place their figure in the center of the room or wherever your crèche is located.

8. Choose an appropriate Christmas hymn to sing together, gathered around the crèche.

9. Then greet each other with the phrase, "Blessed birth!"

Tip: An excellent resource to use in exploring simpler Christmas celebrations is *Unplug the Christmas Machine: A Complete Guide to Putting Love and Joy Back into the Season* by Jo Robinson and Jean Stacheli (New York, Quill, 1991).

FAITH IN ACTION

Giving Tree

During Advent, we can especially be mindful of how we meet Jesus in our world.

> "Come, you that are blessed by my Father, inherit the kingdom prepared for you from the foundation of the world; for I was hungry and you gave me food, I was thirsty and you gave me something to drink, I was a stranger and you welcomed me, I was naked and you gave me clothing, I was sick and you took care of me, I was in prison and you visited me." —Matthew 25:34–36

Jesus often comes to us in the form of those who are needy. How can we be the hands and feet of Jesus to those in need in our communities?

Create a Giving Tree for your home or church community, inviting others to participate in this season of giving. Before the activity contact the leaders of your church's outreach ministries, asking each leader to prepare a list of items desirable for the needy, including inexpensive items, such as toiletries, coffee gift cards, socks, hats, or mittens. You may want to expand this activity to include lists of items from community service agencies.

Materials

- white, unlined 3" x 5" index cards
- Christmas tree
- red ribbon or yarn
- hole punch
- markers

or

- 3' x 6' paper silhouette of a Christmas tree
- Post-it Notes squares
- markers

Directions

1. Write each item desired on a 3" x 5" card and then punch a hole in the corner of each card.

2. Attach the cards to your congregation's Christmas tree by red ribbon or yarn that you string through the holes. Or, if you are using a paper silhouette of a tree, write each item on a slip of Post-it Notes paper and stick the notes to the tree.

WORSHIP

End your celebration singing some Advent hymns. Here are a few suggestions:

O Come, O Come Emmanuel
Come Thou Long Expected Jesus
Hark! A Thrilling Voice Is Sounding
Comfort, Comfort Ye My People

Closing Prayer

Dear God, we fill our days with busy things; things that are necessary and things that are not. Take these precious moments of quiet we offer back to you now, and fill us with what you know we need. (*Silence*) Thank you, God. *Amen.*

Chapter 2

THE ANNUNCIATION

INTRODUCTION

On *The Annunciation of Our Lord Jesus Christ to the Blessed Virgin Mary*, March 25, we celebrate the announcement by the archangel Gabriel to Mary that she is to be the mother of God's Son, Jesus, and Mary's assent in faith to God's invitation (Luke 1:26–38). Gabriel told Mary to name her son *Jesus*, meaning "Savior." Mary's question, "How can this be, since I am a virgin?" is echoed as trust and wonder in her acceptance, "Let it be with me according to your word." According to the Bible (Luke 1:26), the Annunciation occurred "in the sixth month" of Elizabeth's (Mary's cousin) pregnancy with the child later called John the Baptist. While this day falls on our calendar in March, it makes sense to include this celebration as part of our preparation for the coming of Christ during the Advent season.

The Feast of the Annunciation goes back to the fourth or fifth century. Its central focus is the Incarnation: God has become one of us. The term, from the Latin *carnis* ("flesh") literally means "enfleshment." It reflects the christological doctrine that Jesus was fully human and fully divine, the Son of God "in the flesh." It is based on John 1:14, "And the Word became flesh and lived among us." Now, as Luke 1:26–38 tells us, God's decision to walk among us is being realized with Mary's miraculous news. On this day we celebrate the important role Mary had in bringing about the salvation of the world through Jesus Christ. She is a favored one, blessed by God and chosen for a special role.

Who Was Mary?

Mary was a popular name in Jesus' time—there are at least half a dozen in the New Testament. Surprisingly, the Bible has very little to say about this woman held in such high esteem by many Christians, especially in the Roman Catholic Church. Unlike his description of Zechariah and Elizabeth (Luke 1:1–25), Luke makes no reference to Mary or Joseph's faithfulness. Mary is simply "favored," the recipient of divine grace. She's mentioned in the birth of Jesus, the story of finding the twelve-year-old Jesus talking with scholars at the temple, prodding Jesus to perform his first public miracle at the marriage in Cana, in a few brief references during Jesus' ministry, the crucifixion, and at the Holy Spirit's arrival at Pentecost. After Peter's sermon in Jerusalem at Pentecost, Mary disappears from the Bible.

According to ancient Christian sources, Mary was the child of Jewish parents Joachim and Anne and was born in Jerusalem or Sepphoris in Galilee. During her childhood she lived in Nazareth, where she became engaged to the carpenter Joseph, who was descended from King David. If, as the sources suggest and following ancient Middle Eastern customs, Mary was betrothed around the age of fourteen; she was probably born in 18 or 20 BCE.

Joseph, probably considerably older than Mary, disappears from sources soon after he and Mary bring Jesus to the Jerusalem temple to fulfill the Jewish law of Jesus' initiation into the faith. Mary's role also becomes smaller as Jesus' becomes larger. The accounts of Mary's later years, death, and assumption into heaven are found only in traditions outside the Bible, some as late as the fourth century CE. It is not known where she spent her final years, but it is generally believed that she lived with John the son of Zebedee in Jerusalem and died there.

The Virgin Birth

In biblical history, God brought special blessing through children of once barren women, such as Sarah (Genesis 16–21) and Hannah (1 Samuel 1–2). Giving a child to both of these women, who for all natural purposes were effectively dead to be able to give life, shows the power of God to create. There are many parallels in the story of young Mary with these women. Like Sarah and Hannah, Mary's pregnancy is "what the Lord has done for me."

But there are differences. While Sarah and Hannah were very old, with young Mary God is doing a radical, new thing—having a virgin conceive a child by the Holy Spirit. The prophecy of a virgin ("young woman") bearing a son (Matthew 1:22–23) was known to the Jewish people, as foretold in Isaiah 7:14. Mary is the virgin-mother who fulfills this prophecy in a way that Isaiah could not have imagined. She is united with her son in carrying out the will of God (Psalm 40:8–9; Hebrews 10:7–9; Luke 1:38).

Gabriel shares with Mary the role that Jesus will play in God's work of redemption. After naming the child, the angel extends the process of "naming" by offering a glimpse of Jesus' future. Jesus will be called *Son of the Most High* and *Son of God*, titles given to the hoped-for Messiah (2 Samuel 7:14). God will give Jesus the "throne of his ancestor David," and his reign will be endless. Thus he is to be the messianic king foretold by the prophets (Isaiah 9:6–7; Daniel 7:14; Micah 4:7), and he will be sovereign in the kingdom that God is establishing.

When Mary wonders how this will come to pass, reasoning that she is still unmarried, Gabriel describes the miraculous nature of Jesus' conception; it will be by the Holy Spirit. Rather than explaining the "how" of the virgin birth, the angel focuses on the consequences of the Spirit's work in conception:

- Conceived by the Holy Spirit, Jesus will be the Son of God literally—not holy and divine in title only, but in nature also.
- Born of Mary, Jesus will also be human. His birth is not simply an act of God affecting human history but God's entering into human history in flesh and blood.
- Described as being "overshadowed" by the Holy Spirit, Jesus' conception recalls images of creation (Genesis 1:2) and of re-creation (Ezekiel 37:14) and suggests that Jesus will manifest God's creation and redemption.

"Nothing will be impossible with God," echoes God's word to Sarah's laughter about her pregnancy and as well as with Mary, who is blessed both in her faithfulness and in her bearing Jesus. It is indeed a new and miraculous creative act of God, in continuity with those things promised as a new creation in scripture like that of Isaiah 43:19. However, this new humanity is formed within the womb of Mary of earthly material in such a way that the creation is renewed from within. The angel also gives Mary a sign. Her elderly, barren relative, Elizabeth, now awaits the birth of her child. That which seemed impossible comes to pass by the power and grace of God.

Later, when Mary visits her cousin Elizabeth, the baby in Elizabeth's womb leaps, and Elizabeth spontaneously cries out. Luke describes her response as the outward expression of the movement of the Holy Spirit within her. As a result, she identifies Mary as the mother of her Lord, thus confirming the words of Gabriel (Luke 1:35). Elizabeth points to Mary as a model of faith. Twice Elizabeth calls Mary "blessed," for Mary believed the word that was spoken to her from God. In his adult life, Jesus too recognizes that Mary's blessedness does not lie primarily in her role as Jesus' human mother, but in her willingness to believe the word that had been given to her from God (Luke 11:27–28).

Mary responds to Elizabeth's delight with her own joy and rejoicing of God's blessing in what we today recognize as the *Magnificat* (Luke 1:46–55), also known as *The Song of Mary*, found in the Book of Common Prayer, page 50 or 91. Mary's response is one of self-surrender and abandonment to the will of God. "Let it be with me according to your word," she says. Her posture of openness and cooperation in the face of God's loving and gracious advances is the essential attitude of all discipleship.

Roman Catholics teach more than the Virgin Birth. They teach that Mary remained forever a virgin. These conclusions are drawn from early Christian writings, such as the *Protoevangelium of James*, and from early church leaders such as Origen and Athanasius who referred to the "ever-virgin Mary." Mary has an important role to play in God's plan. From all eternity God destined her to be the mother of Jesus and closely related to him in the creation and redemption of the world. We could say that God's decrees of creation and redemption are joined in the decree of Incarnation. Because Mary is God's instrument in the Incarnation, she has a role to play with Jesus in creation and redemption. It is a God-given role. It is God's grace from beginning to end. Mary becomes the eminent figure she is only by God's grace. She is the empty space where God could act.

We Believe

In both the Apostles' Creed and the Nicene Creed we state our belief in Jesus Christ. "For us and for our salvation he came down from heaven: by the power of the Holy Spirit he became incarnate from the Virgin Mary, and was made man." "He was conceived by the power of the Holy Spirit and born of the Virgin Mary."

The conception of Jesus must be understood as an act of God's redemption of the world, and that is why the Spirit is involved. The Spirit, as the perfecting cause of the creation (the *ruach* or "breath" of God) is the agent of the perfecting of Jesus' humanity, through the renewal of the fallen flesh of humankind, which is taken from Mary. "The conception and life of Jesus is a triune act: the Father sends the Spirit to form a body for his Son out of the only material available to hand: the soiled flesh of the created order which he comes to redeem; so that this human life, as a perfect sacrifice of and to God the Father becomes the means of the sacrifice of praise of the whole world."[1]

That the eternal second Person of the Trinity became a human being and "assumed flesh" in Jesus of Nazareth is the core understanding of the Incarnation. Jesus Christ was the "Word made flesh" (John 1:14). The Incarnation holds that Jesus was one divine person with both a divine and human nature. This theology is also used to describe the idea that humans must represent Jesus Christ to others in the world. By God's own act, his divine Son received our human

---

1. Colin E. Gunton, *The Triune Creator* (Grand Rapids: Eerdmans, 1988), 224.

nature from the Virgin Mary, his mother. The divine Son became human, so that in him human beings might be adopted as children of God, and be made heirs of God's kingdom.

Mary's Message Today

While Mary in some ways represents qualities impossible for human beings, especially women, to emulate—ever-virgin yet motherly; always obedient to God's will—her attributes nevertheless represent for many devotees important female properties not provided for by the traditional all-male Trinity. For many, the adoration of a female figure is a vital part of one's faith.

Together with Jesus, the privileged and graced Mary is the link between heaven and earth. She is the human being who best, after Jesus, exemplifies the possibilities of human existence. She received into her lowliness the infinite love of God. She shows how an ordinary human being can reflect God in the ordinary circumstances of life. She exemplifies what the Church and every member of the Church is meant to become. She is the ultimate product of the creative and redemptive power of God. She manifests what the Incarnation is meant to accomplish for all of us.

Celebrating Mary and the Annunciation in your church can lift up the events preceding the birth of Jesus while recognizing how, with God, all things are possible. This celebration takes place nine months before Christmas, allowing us to be "pregnant" with the possibilities that lie ahead for us. The activities in the first section celebrate and inform us about Mary and the role of angels in bringing God's good news. Discovering how God may speak to us through our prayers and encounters with one another, and even strangers, can open us up to new possibilities of how God can work through us—young and old, big and small.

Thus, our Annunciation festivities should include a celebration of our own responsibility to be God's representatives in the world, being open, as Mary would, to God working through us to bring about the reconciliation of the world.

WORSHIP

Opening Prayer

Pray the Collect for the Annunciation (found in the Book of Common Prayer, p. 240):

> Pour your grace into our hearts, O Lord, that we who have known the incarnation of your Son Jesus Christ, announced by an angel to the Virgin Mary, may by his cross and passion be brought to the glory of his resurrection; who lives and reigns with you, in the unity of the Holy Spirit, one God, now and for ever. *Amen.*

Alternatively, you could also read aloud the gospel for the Annunciation of Our Lord, Luke 1:

> In the sixth month the angel Gabriel was sent by God to a town in Galilee called Nazareth, to a virgin engaged to a man whose name was Joseph, of the house of David. The virgin's name was Mary. And he came to her and said, "Greetings, favored one! The Lord is with you." But she was much perplexed by his words and pondered what sort of greeting this might be. The angel said to her, "Do not be afraid, Mary, for you have found favor with God. And now, you will conceive in your womb and bear a son, and you will name him Jesus. He will be great, and will be called the Son of the Most High, and the Lord God will give to him the throne of his ancestor David. He will reign over the house of Jacob forever, and of his kingdom there will be no end." Mary said to the angel, "How can this be, since I am a virgin?" The angel said to her, "The Holy Spirit will come upon you, and the power of the Most High will overshadow you; therefore the child to be born will be holy; he will be called Son of God. And now, your relative Elizabeth in her old age has also conceived a son; and this is the sixth month for her who was said to be barren. For nothing will be impossible with God." Then Mary said, "Here am I, the servant of the Lord; let it be with me according to your word." Then the angel departed from her.

CRAFTS

Angel Mobile

Materials

- white or pastel construction paper shapes of angels (download a pattern at *www.churchpublishing.org/faithfulcelebrations3*)
- shaker bottles of colored glitter or cookie decorating crystals or beads
- white glue or glue sticks
- string or yarn
- paper punch
- thumb tack or sticky tape
- newspaper or box lids
- scissors

Directions

1. Place newspaper on tables or in front of each child.
2. Give each child an angel shape, glue, and their choice of decorating materials. (Children can create their own angel shapes, depending on their ability.)
3. Draw a design or fill in areas of the shape with the glue and then sprinkle materials into the glue. Shake off excess (which you can then pour from the newspaper or box lid back into the container).
4. Punch a hole in the top and tie a length of string or yarn to the top of the angel's head. Attach to the ceiling with a thumb tack or sticky tape.

Annunciation Triptych

The Annunciation has been a major theme in Christian art. A triptych is a work of art (usually a painting) in three sections or panels, all hinged together that can be folded. The word "triptych" comes from the Greek adjective meaning three-fold. Make a triptych of the Annunciation scene, with the Trinity present: Father, Son, and Holy Spirit, as well as Mary, and the Angel Gabriel. Another idea would be to make the figures from clay or play dough, and make a "tableau" using a shallow box to represent Mary's house.

Materials

- 12" x 18" construction paper
- glue
- pencil and markers
- scissors

Directions

1. Fold one piece of construction paper into three sections by taking the right side and folding it to the middle, as well as folding the left side to the middle. You will have three sections of paper. The right and left will be 4.5" x 12" and the middle 9" x 12".

2. Keeping the paper folded (like closed doors), with scissors cut a 4" triangle corner off of both sides of the paper, cutting through all layers. When you open the paper you should have three sections in the form of a "triptych." In medieval times triptychs were painted wood panels depicting scenes from scripture or other stories.

3. Using other pieces of construction paper or markers, design a scene of Mary being visited by the Angel Gabriel, gluing the pieces to the "triptych board."

Celebrate with Flowers

The symbolism of flowers can remind us of Mary and the Annunciation.

Flowers for Mary

In this activity, each participant makes one or more paper flowers. Make several ahead of time to show the examples of each type of flower described below:

Materials

- scissors
- construction paper in bright colors
- yarn
- green pipe cleaners
- glue
- facial tissues in several colors

Directions for Method 1

1. Pinch a paper tissue in the center and twist it several times.
2. These can be formed into a lei by catching the twisted "stem" in a knot along a length of yarn.
3. Or one flower can be attached to the clothes or to a paper headband.
4. Or a pipe cleaner can be twisted onto the base of the flower to form a stem.

Directions for Method 2

1. For each flower, cut three heart shapes from construction paper. (You may want to cut these in advance for small children.)
2. Fold these vertically.
3. Glue one side of each of two hearts to the third heart.
4. Then glue the remaining halves together.
5. Insert a pipe cleaner with a spot of glue on it at the points of the hearts to make stems.

Directions for Method 3

1. Have four heart shapes and one circle cut from construction paper for each flower.
2. Glue four hearts by their points only to the circle.
3. Fold up the heart petals slightly.
4. Attach to pipe cleaner or staple to bulletin board above a drawn-on green stem and leaves.

Centerpieces

Make a flower centerpiece for the dinner table using red carnations (to symbolize *incarnation*), baby's breath (to symbolize *innocence, spirit*) and ivy (to symbolize *eternal fidelity*). Sprinkle the flowers with holy water (little children love to do this), and explain that this consecrates—sets apart—our gift to the worship of God.

Materials

- red carnations
- baby's breath
- ivy
- glass containers for flower arranging—large or small, tall, or short and wide
- green foam floral blocks
- *optional:* floral tape, wire, and sticks

Mary-Golds

Depending on where you live and how temperate your climate is, it might be possible to plant marigolds, named in honor of Mary.

Materials

- seedling pots
- potting soil
- marigold seeds
- newspaper

Directions

1. Spread out newspaper in your work area so soil doesn't spill outside of the activity space.

2. Talk about the waiting that needs to happen to see seeds sprout and grow.

3. Once plants get large enough (and the weather warm enough), transplant the marigolds outside in family gardens or balcony pots.

While you are planting, talk about:

- how the kinds of seeds we are planting are called marigolds, named after Mary, Jesus' mother
- the importance of "hidden" work—as a baby grows unseen within the mother's womb, so a seed grows invisibly under the soil
- how so much that people do for each other is not visible to most people—and perhaps known only to God
- how we need to grow strong in the faith before we can "flower" as God intends us to do

STORYTELLING AND BIBLE STUDY

The Story of the Annunciation

Gather everyone in a circle and read aloud the story of the Annunciation, either the poetic retelling found below, from a children's Bible, or from your favorite Bible translation.

Afterwards, lead a discussion by asking the following questions:

- How do you think Mary felt when the angel told her that her baby would be God's son?
- Why do you think God chose Mary for this important role?

The Story of the Annunciation

Mary was quiet
Mary, the maid of Galilee,
Mary lived by an ancient sea.
She had her dreams, her loves—her life;
she promised Joseph she would be his wife.

Mary grew quiet; Mary grew dark.
She held God's Word as God's own ark.
Mary worked as women did.
She went to the market to shop and bid.
She sat with a spindle and spun sheep's wool.
She baked flat breads and set them to cool.

Mary was quiet; Mary was strong.
She could walk over hills all day long.
As Mary sat and worked one day
she heard God's herald Gabriel say,
"Mary, you are the chosen one
to bear God's Word, to birth God's Son."

Mary was quiet; we cannot know—
Was she afraid? Did she let it show?
"Let what God wants be done to me,"

said Mary, the maid of Galilee.
The angel left. She sat alone.
Did she touch her belly to feel her Son?

Mary was quiet; Mary was strong.
She knew God's Word could heal all wrong.
But did she think God's Word could die?
Did she know his cross? Did she start to cry?
Did she wonder why God would let it be so?
Mary was quiet; we cannot know.

A Story: Mary, Mother of Jesus

Note: This is an especially good story for very young children. Stop to talk over the questions with children.

Do you remember when Jesus was born? Do you remember the name of that special day? What a beautiful day that is for us!

Do you remember the name of Jesus' mother? That's right! Her name was Mary. What are some of the things we remember about her?

Mary lived when there were no cars. How do you think she and her family got around?

She lived when there were no supermarkets where she could buy her bread or food. How do you think she and her family made food to eat?

She lived when there were no department stores to buy her clothes. How do you think she and her family made clothes to wear?

Like all men and women of her day, Mary worked hard.

But her most important work was to say "Yes!" to God when God asked Mary to do something special for all the people in the world. What did God ask Mary to do?

Mary said "yes." Mary became the mother of Jesus. What do mothers do?

Well, Mary did these things for her son, Jesus, and she did them all with love. As a boy, Jesus learned about God's love from his mother Mary.

That is what saints do, you know. Saints want to become God's close friends. They do all the jobs God gives them the best that they can, with deep love in their hearts, and they ask God to help them.

This poem reminds us of what God could have said to Mary:

"Mary, Mary, strong and kind,
Gently rock this child of mine.
Care for him, and tell him too,
Of my love for all of you."

Note: While the poem is recited, children might enjoy rocking an imaginary baby in their arms.

Holy Messengers

In sharing the story of the Annunciation with young children, a simple explanation of this holy mystery can be that God promised to send Jesus to teach us above all to love one another and that Mary was chosen among all women to be his mother. Mary's reaction and response to this Annunciation from God are also very important and send an important message to children about love, faith, and obedience. These can also be topics of discussion when presenting the story.

Christianity is unique in recognizing the Incarnation of the God as Jesus Christ, the Son. God's taking on a human body, while being truly and fully divine, is the reason artistic representations of Jesus, Mary, and others are not "idols" or "graven images" that are prohibited by the First Commandment. When we reverence sacred figures or images we are actually reverencing the person whom the image represents, not the physical object, painting, or sculpture.

Materials

- Bibles (or picture books)

Directions

1. Read about other instances when God sent angels to tell people important messages:
   - Daniel (Daniel 8:15–17)
   - Isaiah (Isaiah 40:1–5)
   - Joseph (Matthew 1:20–21)
   - Zechariah (Luke 1:11–13)
   - the shepherds (Luke 2:8–11)
   - Mary Magdalene (Matthew 28:5–7)
   - Mary (Luke 1:26–38)

2. Compare all these stories of visitation. Who are the messengers?
3. Who are the messengers that come to us today?

Annunciation Discussion and Bible Study

Materials

- Bibles (having various translations available also make Bible study interesting, especially with youth and adults)

Directions

1. Invite someone to read aloud Luke 1:26–56 while everyone else follows along.
2. Compare translations if you choose. Then discuss who Mary was and the role that she played:
   - If Mary is considered the model disciple, what lessons can you learn from her to improve your discipleship?
   - What is God's responsibility in this event? What is Mary's? In what ways is this division of responsibilities true of your relationship with God?

- Compare Luke's account of Jesus' origin with the theological explanation found in John 1:1–18. How do these accounts differ? At what points do they echo one another?
- Read 1 Samuel 2:1–10 and compare Mary's song to Hannah's prayer of thanksgiving. What emotions and attitudes are common to both hymns? What do these songs teach you about God's values? God's ways?
- When have you experienced the "lowliness" of Mary? How has God responded?
- Reread Luke 1:51–53. In the world today, where can you see God exalting the humble, scattering the proud, and sending the rich away empty?

DRAMA

The Magnificat in Story and Dance

This story incorporates a simplified version of Mary's Song of Praise, the *Magnificat* (Luke 1:46–55). Simple dance movements are suggested (in italics) to go with the words. In advance, ask several participants to learn these slow, dramatic movements to teach the other participants. When the actions have been learned, someone can read the story aloud to an audience while the dancers perform.

The Magnificat

My heart praises the Lord,

My soul is glad because of God my Savior.

For God has remembered me, God's humble servant! From now on all people will call me blessed, because of the great things the Mighty One has done for me. Holy is the name of God, who shows mercy to all who honor the Lord.

Begin with all dancers grouped together looking inward. One steps forward and crosses her hands over her heart, raises her arms in praise, then kneels with folded hands as the other dancers place their hands on her head. Then all bow down.

God has stretched out a mighty arm

Dancers raise and stretch their arms as though encircling the world.

and scattered the proud people with all their plans.

All make a slow, dramatic side-to-side sweeping motion.

God brought down mighty kings from their thrones, and lifted up the lowly.

All reach their arms far upward, then bend all the way down as though placing something on the floor. Dancers reverse the last motion.

God has filled the hungry with good things

All pretend to pass food to the children in the audience.

and sent the rich away with empty hands.

All dancers turn away from the audience and walk with out-stretched hands.

God kept the promise made to our grandparents.

All join hands and walk in a circle.

God came to help us and remembered to show mercy to all of us forever!

The dancers form a group, some standing and others kneeling. Raise hands in praise.

Mary and Elizabeth hugged each other and laughed and cried and prayed and shared secrets and talked and talked and talked. Mary stayed with Elizabeth and Zechariah for almost three months; then Mary went back home to Nazareth. She and Joseph had much to do before Mary's own special baby was to be born. But she would never forget this precious time with her cousin Elizabeth.

The dancers can hug one another and show signs of laughter, prayer, and telling secrets to one another. Half the group can then depart from the other, each waving goodbye to each other.

Angel Visitation Role Play

In the activity, take turns reenacting visitations that occurred in the Bible or that might occur today. Participants take turns drawing slips of paper out of baskets and playing the role of the people described on their cards. For each role play, a white card and a colored card are chosen.

Put together a costume box of various objects, hats, robes, angel wings, contemporary clothing, bathrobes, and so on from your Christmas pageant (or Halloween) costume collection. Participants can get "in character" if they choose.

Materials

- 12 white index cards or squares of heavy paper
- 12 colored index cards or squares of heavy paper
- marker, pen, or pencil
- 2 baskets or other form of container like a paper bag or bowl
- *optional:* costume components

Advance preparation

Before the session, prepare the cards and baskets as described here:

1. On the white cards, print "Visitor" on one side of each of them. On the other side of each card write one of the following names along with the message they bring. Leave the remaining cards blank.

   - Gabriel (Bring this message: "You're going to have a baby.")
   - Homeless Person (Bring a message from God.)
   - A Police Officer (Bring a message from God.)
   - Your Best Friend (Bring a message from God.)
   - A Stranger (Bring a message from God.)
   - An Angel (Bring a message from God.)
   - Your Mail Carrier (Bring a message from God.)
   - A Person of a Different Faith (Bring a message from God.)
   - A Child (Bring a message from God.)

2. On the colored cards, print "One Who Is Visited" on one side of each of them. On each individual card write one of the following names or descriptors of a person. Leave the remaining cards blank, which can be offered for adding other roles if you want.

   - Mary, Mother of Jesus
   - A fourteen-year-old young woman in today's world
   - A ninety-year-old man
   - A sixteen-year-old young man in today's world
   - Someone who does not believe in God

- Sarah
- Abraham
- Moses
- Hannah

Play

Two individuals at a time take turns picking a Visitor card or a One Who is Visited card. If they choose, they can use a prop or costume to create their character. (*Note*: They should not tell anyone what is written on their card.) The Visitor begins the dialogue with their message. Let the conversation continue imaginatively!

After each role-play, discuss as a group:

- Who were the characters? How could you tell?
- What happened in this role-play?
- How was each person in the role-play feeling? thinking?

Art Appreciation

An image—such as a painting—can be a wonderful way to bring the beauty and significance of a biblical story to life while also enjoying (or being introduced to) great works art. View some of the most famous and beloved images of the Annunciation by Da Vinci, Botticelli, and Grünewald as well as others perhaps less known (see the list on page 48).

Talk about how these famous painters (make sure to share their names) painted an image of what they imagined when they read the story of the Annunciation. These paintings are hundreds of years old, and people around the world go to museums to admire their beauty. Paintings, no matter when they were created, continue to tell the story of this important event.

Using a computer, the Internet, and an LCD projector, these images can be shared on a screen for a large or small group to view and discuss. A listing of images of art regarding the Annunciation can easily be found at both of these websites:

- *www.textweek.com/art/annunciation.htm*
- *www.wga.hu/*

Discuss

- How would you depict the Annunciation if you were to paint it today?
- What poses would you create for a rendition of Mary's encounter with Gabriel?

List of possible paintings to view

- Fra Angelico, The Annunciation, 1430–32
- Federico Floris Barocci, Annunciation, 1582–84
- Giovanni Bellini, Angel of the Annunciation and Virgin Annunciate, c. 1500
- Daniel Bonnell, Annunciation, contemporary
- Sandro Botticelli, Cestello Annunciation, 1489–90
- Caravaggio, The Annunciation, 1608–09
- Salvador Dali, The Annunciation, 1947
- Garofalo, The Annunciation, 1550
- El Greco, Annunciation, 1595–1600
- Matthias Grünewald, The Annunciation, c. 1515
- He Qi, Annunciation, 2001
- Leonardo da Vinci, Annunciation, 1472–75
- Andrei Rublev, Annunciation, 1405

RECIPES

Angel Cookies

Celebrate the Annunciation of Our Lord with angel cookies. Prepare this simple sugar cookie dough in advance, or purchase refrigerated cookie dough and pre-made icing. Any age can roll out dough, cut out cookies, and decorate after baking. Or bake cookies in advance and have them available for decorating during your celebration.

Ingredients

- ¾ cup sugar
- ½ cup butter, softened
- 1 egg
- ¾ teaspoon vanilla
- 1½ cups flour
- ⅛ teaspoon salt
- ½ teaspoon baking powder
- icing (2 cups confectioners' sugar, 2–3 tablespoons milk, 1 teaspoon vanilla)
- decorations: chocolate sprinkles, colored sugars, etc.

Other supplies

- angel cookie cutters
- measuring cups and spoons
- bowl
- wooden spoon
- mixer
- flour sifter
- rolling pin
- cookie sheet
- rack
- plastic knives and spoons

Directions

1. Put the butter and sugar into a bowl.
2. Use wooden spoon or mixer to cream the butter and sugar together.
3. Beat in the egg and vanilla.
4. In a separate bowl, sift together the flour, baking powder, and salt.
5. Stir the flour ingredients into the butter mixture. (*Note:* The dough will roll out more easily if you allow it to rest in the refrigerator until chilled.)
6. Roll out the dough on a lightly floured surface.
7. Cut out 2" angels with a cookie cutter or with a plastic knife.
8. Put the cookies on a cookie sheet and bake at 325° for about 10 minutes.
9. Put the cookies on a rack to cool.
10. Mix together the confectioners' sugar, the vanilla and the milk to make icing.
11. When the cookies are cool, decorate using icing, sprinkles, colored sugars, etc.

Makes 3–4 dozen cookies.

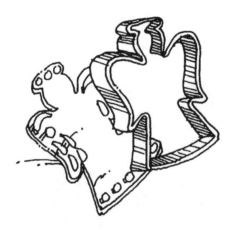

MUSIC

Songs of Mary

"The Magnificat" (Luke 1:46–55) is the song that Mary sings to Elizabeth when they greet one another with joy. This hymn of praise parallels Hannah's prayer of thanksgiving (1 Samuel 2:1–10) and recalls the hymn of deliverance sung by the people of God at the Red Sea (Exodus 15:1–18). In the first part of the song, Mary gives voice to her own experience of God's grace. Written in the first person, these verses focus on God's actions toward Mary.

For Mary, the deliverance of the lowly—now literally acted out in her life—is God's "name" (Philippians 2:5–11). The second part of her song points to the universal implications of Mary's experience. As God has acted toward Mary, exalting her lowliness, so too will God act toward others in the birth of Jesus. God's deliverance equalizes all human relationships (Isaiah 40:4–5). God's deliverance brings hope and salvation to the people of God (Isaiah 61:1–3), fulfilling God's covenant with Israel (Genesis 12:1–3).

There are many songs about Mary in addition to "The Magnificat." Choose one or more of the following to sing together. If possible, discuss the words and what they mean to each person.

These hymns can be found in *The Hymnal 1982:*
- "Ye Watchers and Ye Holy Ones" (682)
- "Lo, How a Rose E'er Blooming" (81)
- "Savior of the Nations, Come!" (54)
- "Of the Father's Love Begotten" (82)
- "Sing We of the Blessed Mother" (278)
- "The Word Whom Earth and Sea and Sky" (263, 264)
- "The Angel Gabriel from Heaven Came" (265)
- "Nova, Nova (Tidings! Tidings!)" (266)
- "Praise We the Lord This Day" (267)
- "Ye Who Claim the Faith of Jesus" (268, 269)

- "Gabriel's Message Does Away" (270)
- "By All Your Saints Still Striving" (for Saint Mary) (232)
- "Sing of Mary" (277)

These can be found in other songbooks and CD collections:
- "Ave Maria" (multiple renditions)
- "Rejoice for Women Brave" (*Voices Found*, Church Publishing)
- "My Soul Proclaims Your Greatness" (Augsburg Fortress)

Note: You may wish to combine this activity with others in this celebration found on pages 42 and 44.

PRAYER ACTIVITIES

Praying with Beads

Major religions have for centuries advocated the use of prayer beads as an aid to prayer. Since the earliest of times, people have used pebbles or a string of knots or beads on a cord to keep track of prayers offered to God.

Originally, a form of repetitive prayer was devised, enabling one to pray while doing routine jobs and between activities. Today, most of us are familiar with the Roman Catholic "rosary," perhaps Hindu "Mala Beads," and Moslem or Buddhist prayer beads.

In recent years, a phenomenon has been circulating in Protestant denominations. Known as the Anglican rosary or Christian rosary, this practice combines elements of both the Orthodox prayer rope ("Chotki") and the Marian rosary.

Beginning in the 1980s, the popularity of these prayer beads has grown rapidly with adults and children as an aid to learning contemplative prayer. Unlike the Catholic rosary of 59 beads and the Hindu "Mala" of 108, Anglican Prayer Beads consist of 33 beads, the number of years in Jesus' life. Grounded in incarnational theology and the Celtic view of the sanctity of all creation, the 33 beads are divided into four sets of 7 beads called "weeks."

The number seven represents wholeness and completion, reminding us of the seven days of creation, the seven days of the temporal week, the seven seasons of the church year, and the seven sacraments. Four larger "cruciform" beads separate the "week," symbolizing the four points of the cross and its centrality in our lives and faith, the four seasons of the temporal year, and the four points on a compass.

A cross is used instead of a crucifix, symbolizing the risen Christ, which is placed next to an "invitatory bead," which serves as an entrance point from the cross into prayer. The use of prayer beads is a very personal invitation to prayer. The prayers said can be recited aloud or in silence, in a group or alone.

There are a variety of prayers that have been written for its use, or one can be spontaneous, using a favorite psalm, scripture passage, or hymn. In using the beads, hold the cross between one's fingers to begin and then move around the beads. The first bead (invitatory) invites us into God's presence, in a similar way as the opening psalm of the Daily Office. Enter the circle of the rosary with one of the four larger beads (cruciform), saying a prayer.

Each small bead can serve as a particular petition or mantra of thanks. A combination of the *Trisagion* ("Holy God, Holy and Mighty, Holy Immortal One") and the *Jesus Prayer* ("Lord Jesus Christ, Son of God, have mercy on me, a sinner") are often used. Continue to pray around the circle, exiting by way of the invitatory bead and cross. This can be repeated as much as one wants, becoming a lullaby of love and praise that allows the mind to rest and the heart to become quiet and still.

Prayer beads use our mental, emotional, and physical nature as well as our spiritual. It leads us to the center of our being—our heart. Feeling the solidness of a bead in one's fingers can help one be mindful of creation and the world, while allowing the repetition of the prayers lead into contemplation. Perhaps because so many of us find it difficult to "quiet one's mind" in today's overactive culture, the tactile aid of holding beads in our hands allows our minds to block out other distractions. They can be held while sitting in traffic, in one's pocket at the grocery store checkout line, or walking on the beach. It can be a powerful meditation tool in which an individual and personal door can be opened to a conversation with God.

Note: There are thirty-three beads, in four sets of seven, with each set separated by a slightly larger "cruciform" bead. Enter the beads through a cross, then an invitatory bead, then the first of the four cruciform beads. Going around the circle, pray through each set of beads and cruciform beads, ending through the invitatory bead and cross again. Two examples are below; others are named above.

Example 1

- Cross: The Lord's Prayer
- Invitatory: Prayer before worship (BCP 833)
- Cruciform beads: Sing or say a verse from a favorite Hymn or Song of Praise
- The Weeks: One prayer for each bead as follows:
    - First set of seven: Adoration
    - Second set of seven: Confession
    - Third set of seven: Thanksgiving
    - Fourth set of seven: Supplication and Petition
- Invitatory: Prayer after worship (BCP 834)
- Cross: The Lord's Prayer

Example 2

- Cross: In the name of God the Creator, God the Redeemer, God the Sustainer, open my heart to your grace and truth.
- Invitatory: Spirit of the living God, come as a gentle breeze and dwell in my heart.
- Cruciform beads: My soul proclaims the greatness of the Lord. My spirit rejoices in God my Savior.
- The Weeks: Holy Jesus, Merciful Redeemer, enfold my spirit within your spirit.
- Invitatory: Spirit of the living God, come as a gentle breeze and dwell in my heart.
- Cross: In the name of God the Creator, God the Redeemer, God the Sustainer, open my heart to your grace and truth.

Making Prayer Beads
Materials

- 28 8-mm beads ("small")
- 4 12-mm beads ("cruciform")
- 1 white stone /10-mm bead ("invitatory")

- 1 stone cross
- 1 32" waxed linen cord

Directions

1. Fold linen cord about ⅓ of the way down and thread folded end through cross, then put loose ends through the loop and pull tight to secure the cross.
2. Tie a little knot near the cross.
3. Put both ends through the white stone invitatory bead and tie another fat little knot above it.
4. Put one end of the cord through one cruciform bead and the other end through the same bead in the opposite direction.
5. Now, on the longer end of the cord, place: • 7 small • 1 cruciform • 7 small • 1 cruciform • 7 small • 1 cruciform • 7 small
6. This makes 4 "weeks" of 7 beads each, divided by the larger bead.
7. Bring the cord you have been working on (now full of beads) back through the first cruciform bead.
8. Adjust the tension of the beads to your liking, and tie a square knot with the two loose ends snugly under the first cruciform bead.
9. Clip ends neatly.

Depending on the size of the beads, all ages can make these (large beads for small children—*be careful of choking hazards!*)

The Rosary

The rosary (from Latin *rosarium*, meaning "rose garden" or "garland of roses") is a traditional Catholic devotion. The term denotes the prayer beads used to count the series of prayers that make up the rosary. The prayers consist of repeated sequences of the Lord's Prayer followed by ten prayings of the Hail Mary and a single praying of "Glory be to the Father" and is sometimes accompanied by the Fatima Prayer; each of these sequences is known as a decade. The praying of each decade is accompanied by meditation on one of the Mysteries of the Rosary, which recall the life of Jesus Christ. The purpose of the rosary is to help keep in memory certain principal events or mysteries in the history of our salvation, and to thank and praise God for them.

To pray the rosary

1. Make the sign of the cross and say the Apostles' Creed.
2. Say the Lord's Prayer (the "Our Father").
3. Say three Hail Marys.
4. Say the Gloria ("Glory be to the Father . . .").
5. Announce the First Mystery; then say the Lord's Prayer.
6. Say ten Hail Marys while meditating on the Mystery.
7. Say the Gloria.
8. Announce the Second Mystery; then say the Lord's Prayer.
9. Repeat steps 6 and 7 and continue with Third, Fourth and Fifth Mysteries in the same manner.

The Hail Mary Prayer

The Angelic Salutation *Hail Mary*, or *Ave Maria* (Latin), is a traditional biblical, Catholic prayer asking for the intercession of the Virgin Mary, the mother of Jesus. The Hail Mary is used within the Roman Catholic Church, and it forms the basis of the rosary. Many other groups within the Western Catholic tradition of Christianity also use the prayer. A somewhat different form of the prayer that omits the explicit request for intercession is used in the Eastern Orthodox and Oriental Orthodox churches and other groups of Eastern Christianity. Some Protestant denominations, such as Lutherans, also make use of some form of the prayer. Most of the text of the Hail Mary can be found within the Gospel of Luke:

> Hail Mary, full of grace, the Lord is with thee; blessed art thou amongst women, and blessed is the fruit of thy womb, Jesus. Holy Mary, Mother of God, pray for us sinners, now and at the hour of our death. *Amen.*

WORSHIP

Conclude your celebration with the following litany or closing prayer from Steve Shakespeare, "The Annunciation," found in *Prayers for an Inclusive Church* (Church Publishing, 2009), 114.

An Annunciation Liturgy Based on Psalm 40:7–11

Leader: Sacrifice and offering you do not desire, but you have given me an open ear. Burnt offering and sin offering you have required. Then I said, "Here I am."

Participants: Here I am, LORD; I come to do your will.

Leader: In the roll of the book it is written of me, "I delight to do your will, O my God; your law is within my heart."

Participants: Here I am, LORD; I come to do your will.

Leader: I have told the glad news of deliverance in the great congregation; see, I have not restrained my lips, as you know, O LORD.

Participants: Here I am, LORD; I come to do your will.

Leader: I have not hidden your saving help within my heart, I have spoken of your faithfulness and your salvation; I have not concealed your steadfast love and your faithfulness from the great congregation.

Participants: Here I am, LORD; I come to do your will.

Leader: Do not, O LORD, withhold your mercy from me; let your steadfast love and your faithfulness keep me safe forever.

Participants: Here I am, LORD; I come to do your will.

Closing Prayer

God of impossible love, announcing to us a new way of being, an unconventional birth: give us the faith of Mary to work with the Spirit of life; give us her perplexity an opening to the event; give us her deep thought which delves beyond the norm; through Jesus Christ, long awaited, unforeseen. *Amen.*

Chapter 3

OUR LADY OF GUADALUPE

INTRODUCTION

The Feast of Our Lady of Guadalupe (*Dia de Nuestra Señora de Guadalupe*) is a celebration of the appearance of the Virgin Mary to an Aztec peasant during the first years of Spanish rule. Today it is both a national and religious holiday in Mexico.

In the early part of the sixteenth century the Spanish conquered the Aztec Empire of present day Mexico. Catholic missionaries swept into the area to convert the indigenous peoples, but often with mixed success. Some decades later, the European Christian faith began to blend with the customs of the Aztec people. One aspect of this was the blending of the veneration of the Virgin Mary in Roman Catholic faith with the Aztec's worship of the goddess Tonantzin. Over the centuries, this evolved into a distinctive Mexican religious culture. The Feast of Our Lady of Guadalupe is one of the best examples of this.

The History of Our Lady of Guadalupe

The Feast of Our Lady of Guadalupe has its origins in December of 1531. Juan Diego, an Aztec peasant who had recently converted to Christianity, was traveling over Tepeyac Hill, the former site of an Aztec shrine to the goddess Tonantzin, about five miles north of present-day Mexico City. What Juan Diego later reported to the local bishop was that he had a vision of the Blessed Virgin Mary as an Aztec maiden and that she had addressed him in his native language. She further asked that a shrine be built in her honor at the site. The local bishop was skeptical and asked Juan Diego to bring a sign of the vision. Three days later, Juan Diego returned to the bishop and produced a bundle of roses from his cloak, on which a colorful image of the Virgin Mary appeared. Stunned by the image and the abundance of roses in the middle of December, the bishop ordered that a shrine be erected. In 1904 the shrine was given the status of a basilica and named the Basilica of Ville Madero.

Today, Juan Diego's cloak, or *tilma*, is displayed above the altar in the Basilica of the Shrine of Our Lady of Guadalupe outside of Mexico City. In 1859 her feast day, December 12, became a Mexican national holiday. Our Lady of Guadalupe is now recognized as the Patroness of Mexico and the Americas. Pope John Paul II also made her the protector of the unborn. To the Aztec people she represented the mother of humankind and the earth goddess.

Historically and emotionally, Our Lady of Guadalupe is deeply woven into the life of all Mexican people. During the wars of independence (1810–12) she was the patroness of the Mexican armies. Almost every Mexican town has a church dedicated to her, and people turn to her for help and guidance on every occasion.

The Celebration of Our Lady of Guadalupe

The festival of Our Lady of Guadalupe, which is a Mexican national holiday, will often begin a week before the feast day of December 12 as pilgrims begin to travel to the Basilica near Mexico City where the most elaborate celebrations are held. The climax of the festival begins on the eve of December 12, when *conchero* dancers gather in the atrium of the church. The dance, composed of traditional hopping or jumping steps performed to the endlessly repeated accompaniment of one or two musical themes, begins at midnight and lasts throughout the day. Groups of dancers alternate to keep up the pace.

This is a very important day for all Mexicans. It is both a religious and national celebration. Both rich and poor enjoy food and drink, and many people will save their money throughout the year for this special celebration.

Ways to Celebrate

In your own observance of this feast day, it is important to remember and teach the difference between the religious celebration and the national celebration of the Mexican people. While the two are intertwined, the distinction is important.

Any celebration should include a liturgy, teaching about the Virgin Mary, Our Lady of Guadeloupe in particular, and a festive meal. Recognition of this feast day for non-Roman Catholics is an opportunity for learning about the Roman Catholic faith and church, and the similarities and differences to your own church.

This feast day of December 12 falls in the midst of the season of Advent. If your church has evening events, this can be the focus of the one for the second week of Advent. You can blend it into your evening celebration by making it the focus of your worship and using some of the activities offered in this chapter. The festive meal also lends itself well to a special Advent evening at church or home.

WORSHIP

Opening Prayer

Sing together the first verse of *Las Mañanitas*, a traditional Spanish "Happy Birthday" song (which has many variations) that people sing early in the morning on birthdays and other special days. Often these songs are used to awaken people on their birthdays. Traditionally this song is also sung as a greeting to Our Lady of Guadalupe either at midnight or at the break of dawn.

Hispanic members of your congregation will likely already know this song, but you'll also find several versions online at a variety of websites, including YouTube. Keep in mind that online version may have some different lyrics. We encourage you to sing the lyrics in both Spanish and English. One YouTube version that *does* feature the lyrics below will be found at *www.youtube.com/watch?v=KUtnS Gyqpm4&feature=related* (use the first verse only).

Las Mañanitas

Estas son las mañanitas	These are the morning songs
que cantaba el Rey David	that King David used to sing.
Hoy porserdía de tusanto	Because today is your birthday
te las cantamos a ti.	We are singing them to you.
Coro:	*Chorus:*
Despierta, mi bien, despierta,	Awaken, my dear, awaken
mira que ya amaneció	and see that the day has dawned,
ya los pajarillos cantan,	now the little birds are singing,
la luna ya se metio.	and the moon has set.

Lady of Guadalupe Prayer Service

The liturgy is the main focus of this Celebration. If you are a non-Roman Catholic Church, this feast may provide an opportunity to work together with a Catholic parish in your community. Perhaps you could hold a joint celebration so that you can experience their liturgy. In any case, plan with sensitivity to the tradition of this festival. In the Catholic tradition, the liturgy includes a celebration of the Eucharist (Communion), and it is appropriate to include this in your liturgical planning as well.

If you will not be offering a traditional Roman Catholic service, model yours on a simple evening prayer service, such as that found on page 61 of the Book of Common Prayer, with the following modifications:

For the readings, use these from the Roman Catholic tradition:
- Zechariah 2:10–13 *or* Revelation 11:19a; 12:1–6a, 10ab
- Luke 1:26–38 *or* Luke 1:39–47

For the Collect of the Day, use this Collect from the Roman Catholic tradition:

> O God of power and mercy, you blessed the Americas at Tepeyac with the presence of the Virgin Mary of Guadalupe. May her prayers help all men and women to accept each other as brothers and sisters. Through Your justice present in our hearts, may your peace reign in the world. We ask this through our Lord Jesus Christ, Your Son, who lives and reigns with you and the Holy Spirit, One God, forever and ever. *Amen.*

Prayer for the Feast

It is tradition to follow the service with a shared meal. As you begin, say the Angelus. This may be prayed in English or Spanish. Make copies of these for everyone to follow along as they pray.

The Angelus (English)

Leader: The Angel of the Lord declared unto Mary

Participants: And she conceived by the Holy Ghost.

Leader: Hail Mary, full of grace: The Lord is with thee. Blessed art thou among women and blessed is the fruit of thy womb, Jesus.

Participants: Holy Mary, Mother of God: Pray for us sinners now and at the hour of our death. *Amen.*

Leader: Behold, the handmaid of the Lord.

Participants: Be it done unto me according to thy word.

Leader: Hail Mary . . .

Participants: Holy Mary . . .

Leader: And the Word was made flesh

Participants: And dwelt among us.

Leader: Hail Mary . . .

Participants: Holy Mary . . .

Leader: Pray for us, O holy Mother of God,

Participants: That we may be made worthy of the promises of Christ.

Leader: Let us pray.

All: Pour forth, we beseech thee, O Lord, thy grace unto our hearts, that we, to whom the Incarnation of Christ, thy Son, was made known by the message of an Angel, may by His Passion and Cross be brought to the glory of His Resurrection, through the same Christ, our Lord, *Amen.*

El Angelus (Español)

Líder: El Angel del Señor anunció a María.

Participantes: Y concibió por obra del Espíritu Santo.

Líder: Dios te salve, María. Llena eres de gracia: El Señor es contigo. Benditatúeres entre todas las mujeres. Y benditoes el fruto de tuvientre: Jesús.

Participantes: Santa María, Madre de Dios, ruega por nosotros pecadores, ahora y en la hora de nuestra muerte. *Amén.*

Líder: He aqui la esclava del Señor.

Participantes: Hagase en mi segun Tu palabra.

Líder: Dios te salve María. . . .

Participantes: Santa María. . . .

Líder: Y el Verbo se hizo carne.

Participantes: Y habito entre nosotros.

Líder: Dios te salve María. . . .

Participantes: Santa María. . . .

Líder: Ruega por nosotros, Santa Madre de Dios.

Participantes: Para que seamos dignos de alcanzar las promesas de Jesucristo.

Todos: Derrama, Señor, Tu gracia en nuestros corazones; que habiendo conocido la Encarnación de Cristo, Tu Hijo, por la voz del Angel, por los meritos de Su Pasión y cruz seamos llevados a la gloria de la Resurrección. Por el mismo Cristo, Nuestro Señor. Amén.

FESTIVE MEAL

For many Mexican families, the celebration of Our Lady of Guadalupe is an opportunity for a traditional family dinner that might include the dishes listed below (though this will vary according to region and family). As community building, the preparation of a group meal is hard to beat. Simple recipes are perfect for engaging young participants, and more involved dishes are a great context for interaction, and a great opportunity for people to feel like they've contributed. What you'll find below are only suggestions; feel free to prepare whatever dishes are familiar and favorites. Again, the Hispanic members of your congregation are your best resource.

A suggested menu for Our Lady of Guadalupe dinner can include refried beans, chicken with mole, rice, salad with mint, watercress, and parsley, and Mexican hot chocolate. (See pages 77–80 for these recipes.) Post a menu listing the items you'll be serving. Decorate the table with a potted poinsettia and an Advent wreath.

Notes

- If time and resources are an issue, many of these dishes can be found already prepared in your local supermarket or Mexican *Mercado*.

- All recipes can be halved.

- You might want to precede the meal with a traditional Mexican soup (*menudo*, for example, or tortilla soup) and follow with flan; these recipes are not provided but readily available online or in many cookbooks.

- To engage all participants, pair younger members with older children or adults. Younger children can hold bowls and stir, while older children often enjoy measuring ingredients.

CRAFTS
Place Cards

Before your Celebration, prepare materials for invitees to create their own place card. When they arrive, ask them to write their names on the cards and decorate them before placing them in front of where they will be sitting at the tables that have been set up in advance.

Materials

- card stock or other heavy paper, cut into 5 x 8 cards (or purchase index cards of this size)
- markers
- stickers: stars, crowns, praying hands, clouds, planets, sun, moon, flowers/roses (all symbols of Our Lady of Guadalupe)

Directions

1. Fold each card in half, lengthwise, to create a "tent."
2. As participants arrive, ask them to write their names in large letters on one side of the "tent."
3. Decorate with stickers and drawings to symbolize Our Lady.

Juan Diego's Cloak

Materials

- participants' coats (if the weather in your location has everyone wearing coats at this time of year)
- assorted art materials (drawing paper, felt markers, crayons, colored pencils, watercolors, etc.)
- poster board
- scissors
- *optional*: garden supply catalogs or gardening magazines that may have roses in them (you may need to collect these in advance during the year when they are available)

Directions

1. Invite everyone to trace the outline of their coat on a sheet of poster board, then cut out the "coat." (Assist younger children as necessary.)

2. Imagine this is the *inside* of Juan Diego's coat, and to decorate it with an image of what they imagine Our Lady of Guadalupe may have looked like. They can also decorate the inside of their coats with pictures of roses (or glue on roses that have been made in the Paper Roses activity found below).

3. Allow time for everyone to share their completed "coats" with the larger group.

Paper Roses

While having real roses at your celebration would be wonderful, it is also fun to make paper roses.

Materials

- tissue paper in various rose colors (pink, red, white, yellow, etc.)
- scissors
- florist's wire or pipe cleaners
- large needle
- *optional:* vase

Directions

1. Stack 4–6 sheets of tissue paper together, and cut them into 4" circles. The size of the circle depends on what size flower you want. An average size would be about 4" in diameter.

2. Leaving the sheets together, fold the circles into quarters and crimp or flute the edges with the scissors. This gives them a more natural look.

3. Using the needle, make a hole in the center of the circles.

4. Cut a 4" piece of the florist's wire and bend it in half. Thread the straight end of the wire through the hole in the tissue papers from front to back.

5. Turn the papers over and gently bunch the circles up around the wire loop. Then easily separate the layers of the tissue paper and pinch and shape them into petal shapes.

6. On the back, or bottom, of the flower, wrap some of the excess wire around the base of the flower to make it secure.

7. You can cut green leaves from construction paper if you like.

8. Arrange the finished flowers into a bouquet or in a vase.

Papel Picado *(Punched Paper)*

Papel picado (punched paper) is a popular art form in Mexico. Its roots reach back to the Aztec culture. The art is still practiced today in many parts of Mexico and the American Southwest. Ancient Aztecs used the bark of wild mulberry and fig trees to make by hand a rough paper called *amatl*. The *amatl* was used to make flags and banners, which the Aztecs used to decorate their temples, homes, and streets.

For this activity, invite participants to make *papel picado* from tissue paper or other hand-made paper much like you would make paper snowflakes. Younger children will need assistance from older children and adults.

Materials

- tissue paper or light-weight handmade paper in 8" x 10" pieces (1 per participant)
- scissors
- string
- tape or glue

Directions

1. Fold the paper 4–5 times, always folding edge to edge not corner to corner. (The less you fold it the easier it will be for young children to cut it.)

2. Cut various shapes into the folded paper using scissors. Do not cut off the corners. The shapes could have significance to this feast or the season of Advent—flowers, stars, etc.

3. Unfold the paper. *Optional:* Crimp or scallop the edges of the paper.

4. Fold the top ¼" of the paper over a piece of string. Glue or tape the edge to mount it securely on the string. Create a decorative banner by placing several on one long string.

5. The completed crafts can then either be used to decorate your space for the festive meal or liturgy activities, or taken home as reminders of the celebration.

STORYTELLING

Telling the Story

Use the following simple summary of the story to provide everyone with some background information about Juan Diego and Our Lady of Guadalupe.

On December 9, 1531, a native Mexican named Juan Diego, who lived a simple life as a weaver, farmer, and laborer, rose before dawn to walk fifteen miles to daily Mass in what is now Mexico City. That morning, as Juan passed Tepeyac Hill, he heard music and saw a glowing cloud encircled by a rainbow.

A woman's voice called Juan to the top of the hill. There he saw a beautiful young woman dressed like an Aztec princess. She said she was the Virgin Mary and asked Juan to tell the bishop to build a church on that site.

Juan Diego went and told the bishop, who was skeptical and asked for proof. But before Juan could go back to where he saw the woman, he found out his uncle was dying, so he hurried to get a priest. However, she met him on the path and told him his uncle had been cured!

The Lady then told Juan to climb to the top of the hill where they first met. He was shocked to find flowers growing in the frozen soil. He gathered them in his cloak, took them to the bishop, explained what had happened, and opened his cloak. The flowers that fell to the ground were Castilian roses—which were not grown in Mexico. But the bishop's eyes were on the glowing image of the Blessed Virgin Mary, imprinted inside Juan's cloak.

Soon after, a church was built on the site where Our Lady of Guadalupe appeared, and thousands converted to Christianity. Juan Diego died on May 30, 1548, at the age of seventy-four.

Note

- Younger children can discover the story through Tomie dePaola's beautifully illustrated book *The Lady of Guadalupe*.
- It would be both fun and educational to show the animated DVD *Juan Diego: Messenger of Guadalupe* (Irving, TX: CCC of America, 2005).

GAME

Be an Explorer

This activity gives everyone the opportunity to learn a little about geography and come away with a "So that's where it all happened . . ." understanding, as they learn more about the place where Juan Diego saw the vision of Our Lady of Guadalupe.

Materials

- digital devices (laptops, tablets, smart phones) with Internet access
- world globe with countries clearly labeled
- map of Mexico (find and print online)
- map of Mexico City and surrounding area (find and print online)

Directions

1. Invite everyone to go exploring to see where the story of Juan Diego and Our Lady of Guadalupe took place.
2. Challenge participants to search for and discuss photos of the Basilica of Our Lady of Guadalupe (both old and new), identify Mexico and its relationship to the United States, find Mexico City, and locate Tepeyac Hill where Juan Diego met Our Lady of Guadalupe.
3. From their online research, calculate the distance from their current location to the location of the story.
4. Everyone can share their findings with the larger, re-gathered group using the maps or globes you also have provided.

DRAMA

History Tableaus

The word *tableau* is short for *tableau vivant,* which is French and means "a living picture." A tableau is the depiction of a scene, usually presented on a stage by silent and motionless costumed participants.

This activity can provide everyone an opportunity to learn about and then express—through simple poses or acting—a bit of the historical context in which the Our Lady of Guadalupe celebration developed. Make available the gathered resources and invite the group to do some research. It may also be helpful to generate a list of questions to help guide and inform their search. Here are some examples:

- When did the Spanish conquest of Mexico take place? Why did the Spaniards come to Mexico? At what Mexican location did the Spaniards first land? Who was the Spaniard Cortez and what role did he play?

- What do we know about the Aztec Empire? What do we know about the Aztec emperor Moctezuma? How did Moctezuma first encounter Cortez?

- What role does Roman Catholicism play in the history of Mexico? What are some differences between Catholicism and Aztec culture? What are the similarities? In what ways does the miracle of Our Lady of Guadalupe reconcile or reflect these differences or similarities?

- How did the symbol of the Virgin of Guadalupe—the "queen of the patriots"— play a part in the Mexican quest for independence? How does the Lady of Guadalupe represent a mix of two blended cultures, both racial and religious? To what does the word *mestizo* refer?

Materials

- digital devices with Internet access (laptops, tablets, smart phones)
- a list of these online sites—just a few among many—may be of some assistance:

  ○ *http://www.mexperience.com/history/conquest.htm*
  ○ *http://en.wikipedia.org/wiki/Spanish_conquest_of
    _the_Aztec_Empire*
  ○ *http://en.wikipedia.org/wiki/Our_Lady_of_Guadalupe*

- materials on Juan Diego and Our Lady of Guadalupe from a
  local library
- information found in the Introduction to this Celebration
- everyday props such as:

  ○ broomstick for a sword
  ○ a garbage can lid for a shield

Directions

1. After everyone has had an opportunity to discover and discuss some of the history and cultural context surrounding the
   veneration of Our Lady of Guadalupe, ask them to select, for
   example, four events that were significant in that time period.
2. After defining these events in the simplest terms possible—for
   example, one event could simply be "the Spaniards invaded
   Mexico"—select a group who can "act" this out by posing their
   bodies to represent the conquest. The members can decide how
   to best represent the scene.
3. Using the simple everyday props provided let the creativity
   flow and encourage participants to have fun remaking history,
   adding their unique slant to the production.

Note: It might be fun to photograph or record the scenes with a digital camera or smart phone to review and show at a later date.

Being Juan Diego

This is an opportunity for pairs of individuals to roleplay Juan
Diego's encounters with Our Lady of Guadalupe. Mixing up ages
as much as possible, one partner takes the role of *Juan Diego* and
the other the role of *Our Lady of Guadalupe*. Partners can decide
whether to reenact Juan's first encounter (in which Our Lady tells
him to build the church) or his second encounter (in which she

fills his cloak with roses and imprints her image on the inside of the cloak). If possible, provide costumes and props to simulate and enhance each character. Each roleplay should take no more than three minutes to present.

Encourage creativity, wonder, and even humor. For example, what questions might Juan Diego have asked? What fears or doubts may he have expressed? In what ways may Our Lady have answered? What might have been the specifics of their conversation?

Give pairs time to prepare, then invite partners to present their roleplays.

After all the roleplays have been presented, invite discussion. If necessary—and as appropriate for participants' ages—you might discuss:

- What sort of man was Juan Diego?
- Do you believe Juan Diego actually smelled roses and heard music? Why or why not?
- Are you skeptical about this or any part of the story? Is it okay to question such things?
- The stories surrounding this vision to Juan Diego indicate that he was very surprised and humbled by the vision. When have you noticed the presence of the Holy or God in your life? Were you expecting it or were you caught by surprise?
- Do you believe God sends messages to ordinary people like you and me?
- When have you felt the presence of something holy— something from God—in your life?
- Were you expecting it or were you caught by surprise?
- Did it affect you or change your life in any way, and if so, how?
- Why do you think the Virgin Mary appeared to him rather than to the local bishop?
- Why was it important that the Virgin Mary resembled the indigenous people in Diego's vision?
- How do these images and this understanding of the Virgin Mary differ from those in our church's tradition? How are they similar?

RECIPES

Make one or more of these recipes for your festive meal described on page 66.

Refried Beans

Serves up to 16.

Ingredients

- 2 pounds dry pinto or kidney beans, rinsed
- 4 tablespoons minced garlic
- 2 medium tomatoes, diced
- 4 tablespoons ground cumin
- 1–2 tablespoons chili powder
- 2 onions, finely chopped
- 4 tablespoons vegetable oil
- salt and pepper to taste

Directions

1. Place beans in large saucepan, and cover with 1 inch of water. Bring to a boil over high heat, then turn off the heat and allow the beans to sit for 1 hour.
2. Drain beans and cover with fresh water.
3. Stir in 1 tablespoon of garlic, the tomato, cumin, and chili powder.
4. Bring to a boil over high heat, then reduce and simmer until the beans are very soft, about 1½ hours. Add water as needed. Once the beans have cooked, remove and mash half of the beans.
5. Heat the oil in a large frying pan and add the onion. Cook until translucent but not soft.
6. Add the whole and mashed beans, along with the remaining garlic. Add salt and chili powder if desired. Cook the beans, stirring often, until heated through. Add additional water to achieve the desired consistency.

Chicken with Mole

Serves up to 16.

Ingredients

- ½ cup vegetable oil
- 8 onions, finely chopped
- 4 pounds tomatoes, chopped (or 2 28-ounce cans of chopped tomatoes with the juice)
- 8 hot chile peppers, minced (or 4–8 tablespoons of dried chili flakes)
- 4 tablespoons finely chopped fresh cilantro
- ground black pepper to taste
- 2 teaspoons white sugar
- 12 skinless, boneless chicken breast halves
- 1 cup chopped fresh oregano
- 2 teaspoons ground cinnamon
- 4 teaspoons ground cumin
- 4 bay leaves
- 8 squares (8 ounces) unsweetened chocolate
- juice of 1 lime
- ½ cup chopped fresh parsley or cilantro (for garnish)
- 8–12 cups cooked rice

Directions

1. Heat the oil in a Dutch oven over medium heat. Cook onions until translucent, then stir in the tomatoes, cooking and stirring until they release their juice.
2. Stir in the chile peppers, cilantro, black pepper, and sugar. Bring to a boil and cook for about 10 minutes until thickened.
3. Add chicken, oregano, cinnamon, cumin, bay leaves, chocolate, and lime juice. Stir to blend and simmer over medium heat for 15 to 30 minutes—or until chicken pieces are cooked through.

4. Remove bay leaves. Serve chicken smothered in sauce over rice. Garnish with additional fresh parsley or cilantro.

Salad with Mint, Watercress, and Parsley

Serves up to 16.

Ingredients

- 1½ cups olive oil
- 6 tablespoons lemon juice
- salt to taste
- ¼ teaspoon freshly ground pepper or to taste
- 2 cloves garlic, minced (*optional*)
- 2 small heads romaine lettuce, washed and torn into small pieces
- 2 small heads red leaf lettuce, washed and torn into small pieces
- 2 bunches fresh flat-leaf (Italian) parsley, stems removed
- 2 bunches fresh mint, stems removed
- 4 watercress bunches, stems removed

Directions

1. For the dressing, whisk together the oil, lemon juice, garlic, salt, and pepper in a small bowl.
2. In a salad bowl, combine the romaine, red lettuce, parsley, mint, and watercress.
3. Drizzle the dressing over the greens. Toss to coat.

Mexican Hot Chocolate

Serves up to 12.

Ingredients

- ½ cup unsweetened cocoa
- ½ cup white sugar

- 1½ teaspoon ground cinnamon
- 8 cups milk
- 1 cup cream
- 1½ teaspoon vanilla extract

Directions

1. In a small bowl whisk together the cocoa, sugar, and cinnamon.
2. Heat 1 cup of milk in a saucepan *until just beginning to bubble*—watch it closely (do not boil). Remove from heat.
3. Slowly add the hot milk to the cocoa mixture, whisking until smooth. Return the chocolate milk mixture to the saucepan, and place it over the heat again. Allow it to just come to a boil over low heat. Stir in the remaining 3 cups of milk, and again return just to boiling.
4. Before serving, whisk until frothy, stir in the cream and vanilla. Serve hot.

WORSHIP

Closing Prayer

Repeat the first verse of Las Mañanitas, which today's celebration began. Once again, sing it in honor of Our Lady of Guadalupe.

Estas son las mañanitas	These are the morning songs
que cantaba el Rey David	that King David used to sing.
Hoy porserdía de tusanto	Because today is your birthday
te las cantamos a ti.	We are singing them to you.
Coro:	*Chorus:*
Despierta, mi bien, despierta,	Awaken, my dear, awaken
mira que ya amaneció	and see that he day has dawned,
ya los pajarillos cantan,	now the little birds are singing,
la luna ya se metio.	and the moon has set.

Chapter 4

LAS POSADAS

INTRODUCTION

Posadas is Spanish for "inns" or "lodgings." Las Posadas is a nine-day celebration of Mary and Joseph's journey to Bethlehem and their search for lodging along that journey.

In Mexico, in contrast to many Western countries, the celebration of the Christmas season has remained a highly religious holiday centered around the celebration of the birth of Jesus. Santa Claus, Christmas trees, and many of the things that we associate with Christmas in the United States are not as prevalent, if they are present at all. The Christmas celebration begins on December 16 with Las Posadas and lasts for nine days leading up to the festival Mass on Christmas Eve. Gift giving is on January 6, the Feast of the Epiphany, when the magi arrived with their gifts for the Christ Child.

Typically, Las Posadas is a neighborhood celebration. Every home will have a Nativity scene. Each evening a candlelit procession of all ages moves through the neighborhood, stopping at different houses to request lodging. After two stops, and being turned away two times, they arrive at the third house that invites them in "for the night." The stops along the way are pre-determined as is each evening's host home.

The hosts of the home are the innkeepers, and the neighborhood children and adults are *los peregrinos*, the pilgrims, who have to request lodging through singing a simple chant (see below). Older teenagers will typically carry small statues of Mary and Joseph at the front of the procession. There is often a lantern at the head of the procession also.

The singing of the song, or chant, goes back and forth between those outside and inside the house until the innkeeper decides to let the travelers in. Those outside are singing the part of Joseph asking for shelter, while those inside are singing the part of the innkeeper.

Once admitted to the third house there are special prayers (in Mexico that usually includes the recitation of the rosary), perhaps a Bible reading, and then the party can begin. The party can be a simple get-together to something larger with food and games. For the children there will be a piñata that has been filled with dried and fresh fruits and nuts. The piñata may or may not contain candy.

Ways to Celebrate

Choosing to recognize and celebrate Las Posadas provides your community with a wonderful opportunity to learn more about Mexican culture and history. If you choose to separate people by ages, adults and older youth benefit from a speaker who is native to the culture. You should try to make the presentation as interactive as possible, perhaps with the use of maps, videos, clothing, and food. For younger children storybooks are effective as are short video presentations. Again, simple maps are helpful as are foods and clothing.

Because *Faithful Celebrations* is meant to provide your church with single celebrations, the plan that follows assumes you will gather just once to celebrate Las Posadas. However, this festival can be celebrated in neighborhoods where members of your congregation live over the entire nine days from December 16–24, or it could be shortened to fewer evenings. You will want to be sensitive to the cultures in your church, town, and neighborhoods. And if you have a high Mexican presence (in your church and/or your neighborhood), celebrate and take advantage of this by inviting them into your planning and the final festival.

Our Las Posadas processes through your church with three rooms designated as the inns. Within each inn different families, small groups, or individuals serve as hosts/innkeepers. It could be particularly effective if done near Christmas Eve or on Christmas Eve itself. The third stop could be expanded to include a dinner for all. And remember—invite the stranger and those who are alone.

The celebration involves three parts: First, you will make preparations for Las Posadas, including creating a piñata, preparing food, and learning the chants; second, you will enact Las Posadas; third, all ages will be given an opportunity to reflect on their experience. For the first part, divide into groups as appropriate for various ages, but try to combine ages as you prepare the various materials for the actual procession. Keep in mind that with some help and careful supervision, even the youngest participants can take part in most activities.

Pre-planning is needed before your event. In particular, you should answer these questions:

- What route will our procession follow?
- What rooms will be the three lodging stops? Once these are determined, let smaller groups, families, and individuals plan how they will enact their parts. For example, will they dress in costume? Will certain roles be assigned to specific people?
- For the room that is chosen as the third and final lodging, determine the food to be provided, party activities (especially for children), who will play the roles of Mary and Joseph, who will lead the chanting at the doors, will people carry candles or lanterns, etc. For the food, costumes, and games, assign these to different small groups, individuals, or families to plan and prepare. This increases involvement and enthusiasm for the event itself.
- Music should be planned in consultation with your organist/ choir director if possible. Not only does this provide you with a wonderful opportunity to work together, but it involves more people in the planning, promotion, and attendance while giving you access to a greater wealth of musical options. Involving instruments other than the organ, such as guitars, would allow your music to travel with you from "house to house."

Beyond the Celebration

Because Las Posadas is about Mary and Joseph's search for lodging, and finding none, you may wish to study about homeless shelters and community housing in your town. Can you bring in a speaker? Are there volunteer opportunities? Can your church become housing for the homeless for a certain week during the winter? What government agencies in your area deal with the homeless and how might church or family members offer to help?

WORSHIP

Opening Prayer

Pray the Collect for Christmas Day (found in the Book of Common Prayer, p. 212):

> O God, you have caused this holy night to shine with brightness of the true Light: Grant that we, who have known the mystery of that Light on earth, may also enjoy him perfectly in heaven; where with you and the Holy Spirit he lives and reigns, one God, in glory everlasting. *Amen.*

Invite participants to sing together a beloved Christmas carol. "O Little Town of Bethlehem" is a good option, as is the traditional Mexican song "Los Peregrinos" ("The Pilgrims"). You can find the music with lyrics, in both English and Spanish, at *http://cnx.org/content/m12609/latest/.*

Follow the singing with the following piece of scripture:

O Gracious Light *Phos hilaron* (from the Book of Common Prayer, p. 118)

O gracious Light,
pure brightness of the everlasting Father in heaven,
O Jesus Christ, holy and blessed!

Now as we come to the setting of the sun,
and our eyes behold the vesper light,
we sing your praises, O God: Father, Son, and Holy Spirit.

You are worthy at all times to be praised by happy voices,
O Son of God, O Giver of life,
And to be glorified through all the worlds.

The Song of Mary (The Magnificat, Luke 1:46–55)

See page 44

CRAFTS

Piñatas

Depending on the number of participants, you may want to make one or several piñatas in advance of your Celebration. It's best to give everyone a chance to take a swing or two to try to break them open.

Materials

- several large paper grocery bags
- dried fruit in Ziploc-style clear bags (While candy is not traditional in Las Posadas celebrations, it is your choice on whether or not to include it. Nuts are typically included, but due to allergies, it is safe to eliminate the use of them today. You could also include some simple nonfood gifts such as art supplies, bracelets, etc.)
- tissue paper in bright colors
- newsprint
- thinned craft glue
- wide paint brush
- craft glue
- scissors
- tape
- stapler
- hole punch
- colored yarn or string
- assorted decorations, such as glitter, sequins, rickrack, stickers, etc.
- stick, board, or a broom handle (to be used after the meal to break open the piñatas)

Directions

1. Place an opened bag on a table. Into the bag place several handfuls of the fruit, candy, and other items that you have selected. Scrunch up some clean, blank paper (such as newsprint) on top of the contents, leaving about 2" at the top of the bag for easy closing.

2. Roll the top of the bag closed (rolling it several times) and staple shut.

3. Wrap the bag in several layers of tissue paper, which helps reinforce the bag and make it a harder to break open. Brush the tissue paper with a layer of thinned glue to help it stick.

4. After a few minutes of drying time, let participants decide how they want to decorate the piñata. It could be painted to resemble an animal or a flower. Or lots of strips of tissue paper can be glued to the outside of the bag to make it colorful and festive. It's fun to have some of the strips of tissue paper hang down from the bottom of the bag.

5. When you are finished decorating the bag, punch two holes in the top of the bag, about an inch from the corners. Take a 3-foot piece of the yarn or string, and put it through the hole on one end and run it to the other end. (This is for hanging the piñata, so leave as much slack as you will need.) Tie the knots at the two ends securely. Your piñata is ready to hang!

6. Repeat the process if you plan to have several piñatas to break during your celebration.

7. Hang the completed piñatas in the final inn of the procession.

STORYTELLING AND BIBLE STUDY

Any of the following suggestions for learning about the tradition of Las Posadas and its biblical roots can be done before or after your procession and festive meal. Choose the timing and activities according to how you have planned your event to fit your own needs.

The Story of Las Posadas

Children of all ages can learn about the tradition of Las Posadas from the sharing of picture books about this festivity. At the beginning of your celebration it might be appropriate to introduce the story behind this festival. Provide an area where books are available for children (or teens and adults) to relax and read some stories if you don't what to share a story with your whole group together. Here are some resources your local library may have available:

For children

- Tomie dePaola's *The Night of Las Posadas*
- Virginia Kroll and Loretta Lopez's *Uno, Dos, Tres, Posada!*
- Diane Hoyt-Goldsmith and Lawrence Migdale's *Las Posadas: An Hispanic Christmas Celebration*

For youth and adults

- *World Book Encyclopedia's Christmas in Mexico*
- Susan Weber's *Christmas in Santa Fe*
- Rafaela G. Castro's *Chicano Folklore: A Guide to the Folktales, Traditions, Rituals and Religious Practices of Mexican Americans*

If you read any of these stories after your procession, you might ask:

- What's your favorite part of today's story?
- What parts of the story did you not like?
- What do you like most about Christmas?
- Is there something about Christmas you do not like? What is that?

- What did you most enjoy about out time together tonight (today)?

Reflecting on the Story

This would be most effective if done *after* your procession. Invite youth and adults to sit together in a circle. Invite a volunteer to read aloud the story of Mary and Joseph's arrival in Bethlehem from Luke 2:1–7, the gospel story upon which Las Posadas is based.

The Birth of Jesus

In those days a decree went out from Emperor Augustus that all the world should be registered. This was the first registration and was taken while Quirinius was governor of Syria. All went to their own towns to be registered. Joseph also went from the town of Nazareth in Galilee to Judea, to the city of David called Bethlehem, because he was descended from the house and family of David. He went to be registered with Mary, to whom he was engaged and who was expecting a child. While they were there, the time came for her to deliver her child. And she gave birth to her firstborn son and wrapped him in bands of cloth, and laid him in a manger, because there was no place for them in the inn.

Discuss

- How did you feel as you were rejected during our procession?
- How did you feel when you were finally accepted?
- How do we make room for Jesus in our lives today?
- When is it hard to make room for Jesus? When is it easy?
- In our daily lives—at home, at school, at work, with friends— when do we have opportunities to welcome strangers? Or people who might be lonely, sad, or frightened?

Spinning the Story

Materials

- Bibles
- whiteboard or newsprint with markers
- a variety of art supplies, including poster board, markers, paints, modeling clay, scissors, construction paper, glue, old magazines and newspapers, etc.
- writing supplies, including paper and pens or pencils
- video recorder and monitor (or computer)

Directions

1. Explain to those gathered that you will be reading aloud the text of Luke 2:1–7, on which Las Posadas is based (see page 90).

2. Invite everyone to close their eyes and form mental images of the story as it moves along. Try to picture what each character and each place in the story looks like.

3. After the reading, ask participants to describe their idea of each character. Ask:

    - What does he or she look like?
    - How do they act?
    - Why do they do what they do?

4. Keep notes on the whiteboard or newsprint of group members' observations.

5. Then, challenge participants to create and tell the story in a different way using contemporary images and motifs. The simplest idea would be to create contemporary travelers seeking lodging at roadside motels, but invite participants to recast the story even further than that. Perhaps it's a story about coming to a new school and finding the first friendship that allows a spirit of welcoming and acceptance. Maybe it's a story about trying unsuccessfully to connect with social rivals and

eventually finding community. Maybe it's a story about less-is-more and the discovered value of humble surroundings and valued friendships.

6. Invite individuals, pairs, or small groups to create art that communicates this new, contemporary version of the story told in Luke 2:1–7, using any of the available art or writing supplies. Participants could paint, sculpt, draw, write, or record their understandings and ideas.

7. Once they've completed their projects, invite volunteers to share their completed artwork with the entire, re-gathered group before the Celebration's closing prayer.

Identifying with the Story

Materials

- Bibles

Directions

1. Gather together in a circle. Ask a volunteer to read Luke 2:1–7 aloud (see page 90).

2. Discuss:

   - Who are you in the story?
   - Who else from your contemporary life is in the story?
   - What part of the story speaks most directly to you?
   - What do you think that God is saying to us in this story?
   - How would you change or add to the story to help make its point?
   - What do you think that Joseph would say was Mary's biggest concern?
   - What do you think that Mary would say was Joseph's biggest concern?
   - What is the story saying specifically to people in your age range? How would you describe the message?

DRAMA

Preparing Costumes

While it isn't necessary to dress in any particular way to participate in Las Posadas, it may add to the experience to dress as the biblical characters going from house to house seeking shelter.

Materials

Towel/Necktie to cover head

Rope tie at waist

Bathrobe

- a variety of clothing that could pass as "biblical," for example, bathrobes, twin bed sheets, scarves, sandals, rope belts, towels for head-coverings, old ties, etc.

- Christmas pageant costumes

Directions

1. Make available the collected materials and invite each participant to create his or her own costume.

2. Just adding one or two items can create an illusion. For example, a towel wrapped around the head and tied with a necktie makes a serviceable head covering.

Learning the Chants

Once you've decided who will be the pilgrims traveling from inn to inn, and who will be in the inn (innkeepers and lodgers), it's time to teach each group its chant.

Materials

- copies of the chant noted below (download at *www.church publishing.org/faithfulcelebrations3*) for each of three groups (pilgrims, innkeepers, lodgers)

Directions

1. Divide everyone in to three groups: pilgrims (who will travel), innkeepers (who are at each stop), and lodgers (who are inside the third "inn").
2. Distribute the appropriate chant to each group.
3. Encourage groups to practice their chants so they'll be able to recite them easily and in unison.

*At each house, the **pilgrims** chant:*

> In the name of heaven
> I ask you for lodging,
> because she cannot walk,
> my beloved wife.

*The **innkeepers** at the first two inns will answer:*

> This is no inn,
> So keep on going.
> I won't open the door,
> in case you are robbers.

*At the third (final destination) inn, those **lodgers inside** chant:*

> Enter, holy pilgrims!
> Accept this dwelling—
> not of this humble house,
> but of my heart.

RECIPES

Preparing the Meal

While you have the freedom to plan and choose whatever foods you'd like, this is a perfect opportunity to mix Western and Mexican foods. Depending on the timing of your Celebration, you may want to provide a complete dinner (if gathering in the evening) or only snacks (if gathering for an afternoon). In any case, be conscious of people's differing tolerance for spiciness!

In addition to the punch mentioned below (*Ponche Navideño*, or Party Punch), tamales are a common food at a Mexican Las Posadas, as are fruit salads. Some things to consider as you work together to prepare the meal:

- Let everyone share in the tasks, assigning the simplest tasks to the youngest participants.
- Always provide adult supervision around hot stoves and electrical equipment.
- Consider pairing older participants (adults and youth) with children, giving them specific tasks to accomplish together.
- Find a way to keep the warm foods warm and the cold foods cold until ready to start your Las Posadas feast.

Depending on timing, you may want to set the food up in the final inn, ready for the feast. If you are holding your procession in your church or a home, it will likely take no longer than 15–20 minutes. Or you can wait to bring the food in once the pilgrims have finished their walk to the final inn.

Ponche Navideño (Party Punch)

Ponche Navideño is a traditional Mexican Christmas punch—a hot, sweet drink made from seasonal fruits and cinnamon sticks. For adults, this punch often contains a shot of alcohol, commonly tequila, rum, or brandy (this would be the *con Piquete*, or "punch with a sting").

Ingredients

- 8 quarts water
- 1 lb. *tejocotes* (small golden apples—though color can range from red-orange to a translucent golden yellow—with a sweet and sour taste, reminiscent of something between a plum and an apricot)
- 3 whole oranges
- 8 guavas
- 2 pounds sugar cane
- 1 pound pitted prunes
- 3 pears
- 1 cup raisins
- 6 ounces walnuts, coarsely chopped
- 3 sticks cinnamon
- ½ cup whole cloves
- 2½ pounds *piloncillo**

Directions

1. In a medium saucepan, bring 1 quart of water to a boil. Add the tejocotes, lower the heat and simmer for 6–8 minutes until softened. Remove the fruit, then peel and cut off the hard ends.

2. Peel the sugar cane and slice it into medallions. Remove the stems and cores from the pears and cut into large chunks. Cut the guavas and prunes in half. Stud the oranges with the whole cloves. Cut the cone of piloncillo into large chunks.

3. In a very large pot, bring the remaining 7 quarts of water to a boil. Add all the fruits and nuts to the pot and bring back to a boil.

4. Lower heat and simmer for approximately 30 minutes, stirring gently and occasionally. Add the piloncillo and cinnamon. Simmer for another 30 minutes.

5. Remove from heat. Ladle into cups, making sure each gets some chunks of fruit and nuts.

6. Serve hot . . . but not too hot. Be sure to test the temperature before serving to children.

Makes about 30 servings.

Note: Piloncillo is Mexican raw sugar shaped into hard cones. Smaller chunks are sometimes labeled *panocha.* You may be able to get them in a market that sells Hispanic foods. If neither is available, substitute an equal weight of packed dark brown sugar.

Las Posadas Fruit Salad

Ingredients

- apples
- oranges
- grapes (red and green)
- bananas
- nuts (walnuts, pecans, and/or almonds)
- heavy cream
- sugar
- *optional:* cooked beets and chopped, raw jicama

Directions

1. Clean and chop equal portions of fresh apples and oranges. The amount will depend, of course, on the number of people expected at your celebration.
2. Combine in a large bowl and add bananas, grapes (green and red), and nuts. (For a more traditional version of this salad, add chopped, cooked beets and chopped, raw jicama.)
3. To make the dressing, combine heavy cream and sugar to taste (again, judging the amounts by your amount of fruit).
4. Pour the dressing over the salad about 30 minutes before serving. These are traditionally garnished with fresh poinsettia leaves. (However, while poinsettia leaves are not poisonous,

their bad taste may cause vomiting. If you choose to use them as a garnish, make sure children—or anyone—know they should not to be eaten.)

Easy Tamales

Homemade tamales typically consist of cornmeal dough, rolled with ground meat or beans usually seasoned with chili, wrapped in corn husks, and steamed. The recipe below is a streamlined version that's quick, easy, and still quite tasty.

Ingredients

- 2 pounds ground beef
- salt and pepper, to taste
- onion, as desired
- 2 cans chili (with or without beans)
- 4 cans cream of mushroom soup
- 2 twelve-count packages of small, flour tortillas
- 16 ounces shredded cheddar cheese

Directions

1. Brown the ground beef and onion, seasoning with salt and pepper.
2. Pour off grease.
3. Add chili and soup to the meat mixture, heating through.
4. Place a small amount of the meat mixture on the bottom of two 9" x 13" pans to flavor the tamales while they bake.
5. Spoon about ⅓ cup of meat mixture onto the middle of a tortilla, fold in half, and place in the pans on top of the thin coating of meat mixture.
6. Continue to fill shells and place in pans, overlapping a bit and making one layer.
7. Sprinkle some cheese on shells.

8. For the second layer, follow the same steps as for the first layer, but layer the tamales in the opposite direction. Again sprinkle with cheese.

9. Pour remaining meat mixture over the top. Top with cheese.

10. Cover with foil and bake at 350° for 20 minutes.

Makes about 24 servings.

THE PROCESSION

By now you are ready for your Las Posadas procession! You've chosen your inns, the costumes are ready, the chants are practiced, the food is prepared, and the piñata is ready and waiting. The work is over . . . now for the fun.

Materials

- costumes
- chant cards
- electric lanterns (safest) or candle lanterns (held by adults or youth)
- the food prepared for the feast
- napkins, placemats, utensils, serving utensils, etc.
- piñatas
- stick, board, or cane for breaking the piñatas
- blindfolds

Directions

1. Begin by getting into costume (if you haven't already). Then ask your innkeepers (all three sets or individuals) to take their places in their various inns. The doors to each inn should be closed.

2. Remaining participants— *los peregrinos*, the pilgrims—gather and begin singing as they make their way to the first of the three inns.

3. When the pilgrims arrive at the first inn, they chant (two or three times):

In the name of heaven
I ask you for lodging,
because she cannot walk,
my beloved wife.

4. The innkeeper(s) at the first inn chant (two or three times), through the door:

This is no inn,
So keep on going.
I won't open the door,
in case you are robbers.

5. The pilgrims, with sad faces, start singing again and walk to the second inn. There they again chant (two or three times):

In the name of heaven
I ask you for lodging,
because she cannot walk,
my beloved wife.

6. The innkeeper(s) at the second inn chant (two or three times), through the door:

This is no inn,
So keep on going.
I won't open the door,
in case you are robbers.

7. The pilgrims, again with sad faces, start singing again and walk to the third and final inn. There they again chant (two or three times):

In the name of heaven
I ask you for lodging,
because she cannot walk,
my beloved wife.

8. At the third (final destination) inn, those inside open the door and chant (two or three times):

Enter, holy pilgrims!
Accept this dwelling—
not of this humble house,
but of my heart.

9. As the pilgrims (and the innkeepers from the first two inns) enter, they sing joyfully together either "O Little Town of Bethlehem" or the traditional Mexican song "*Los Peregrinos*" ("The Pilgrims").

10. Then begin the feast!

After eating, clear a large enough area for the breaking of the piñatas. Demonstrate how this process works with a child at least eight years old. Blindfold the child, stand him or her beneath a piñata, spin the child (gently) once or twice around, stand back, and ask them to take two or three swings to try to hit or break open the piñata. If they succeed, everyone can scramble to grab a few of the treats. If the piñata does not break, another child gets a chance.

After this first attempt at breaking open the piñata, start with the youngest group members and work upward from there.

Please exercise caution during the piñata portion of the celebration. Make sure everyone (and anything breakable) is well out of reach of the stick as it's being swung.

WORSHIP

Closing Prayer

If possible, conclude today's celebration in your darkened church, perhaps by candlelight. A Compline service would be a contemplative way to quiet down after the evening's (or afternoon's) excitement.

Use a service from your own denomination's book of worship. You'll find a Compline service in the Book of Common Prayer starting on page 139. The service could be shortened to accommodate young children.

A simpler option is to sit together in a circle on the floor in your third inn, where you have held your feast. Invite volunteers to share what they liked most (or what they learned) from today's celebration of Las Posadas. Close with a simple prayer such as this, also from the Book of Common Prayer (p. 124):

Lord Jesus, stay with us, for evening is at hand and the day is past; be our companion in the way, kindle our hearts, and awaken hope, that we may know you as you are revealed in scripture and the breaking of bread. Grant this for the sake of your love. *Amen.*

Chapter 5

CHRISTMAS

INTRODUCTION

Our Christmas liturgy is drawn from two ancient traditions, that of the Eastern Church and that of the Western Church. The Eastern Church's incarnational liturgy emphasized the manifestation of God in Jesus, making Epiphany, observed in January, the chief incarnational feast with its own traditions and significance.

In contrast, the Western Church's incarnational liturgy emphasized the humble birth of Jesus at Bethlehem, making Christmas, December 25, the chief incarnational feast. The Church picked this date to coincide with a pagan festival celebrating the return of light at the winter solstice. Hence, many of the prayers at Christmas draw a parallel between Christ's birth and the gift of light—the true light—that he brings. Western culture—from the most sophisticated art to the humblest folk custom—has retained this Christmas focus on the birth at Bethlehem. This focus has given rise to many traditions such as Christmas trees, gift giving, and nativity pageants.

A Day and a Season

The Church gives us time to enjoy all these traditions by making Christmas more than a day but a season. Christmas season begins with first vespers of Christmas and ends with the feast of the Baptism of the Lord on the Sunday after Epiphany. The full observance of the Christmas season, and the preservation of our traditions, can help us keep the Christmas celebrations of our families and congregations centered on Jesus.

The season is enriched by one feast after another. The Feast of the Holy Innocents on December 28 and the Feast of the Holy Name on January 1 are part of the Christmas season. Of course, January 1 is also the civil New Year, which can serve to remind us that God's salvation redeems all time.

Tips for Leaders

Consider making your Christmas celebration a birthday party for Jesus, complete with birthday cake and decorations.

Most people enjoy sharing their favorite family foods during the holidays. Ask participants to bring their favorite Christmas treat to share.

You also might want to set aside time for Christmas caroling in the neighborhood near your home or church.

Beyond the Celebration

If you'd like to extend the celebration into the week ahead, here are several additional options:

- Plan a group outing to go Christmas caroling at the homes of those who are homebound in your congregation or neighborhood, taking food items or other practical gifts that would be appreciated. You might also visit a nursing home, crisis shelter, food pantry, or other community service location.

- Invite participants to serve food to the hungry. If your congregation has no such ongoing ministry of its own, contact organizations in the community that do. If possible, include children if the organization is open to their participation.

Celebrating the World Community

Christmas is, obviously, a worldwide celebration. You can bring this home to group members—and enhance your celebration—by inviting participants (in advance) to be ready to sing together a simple carol (such as "Silent Night") in whatever language represents their ethnic background: Dutch, Spanish, German, Polish, Italian, Japanese, or more.

Similarly, ethnic food for Christmas is especially popular, and no Christmas gathering would be complete without sharing it. Invite participants to bring food, recipes, and stories about family celebrations from times past.

WORSHIP

Opening Prayer

Offer this prayer, the "Collect for the First Sunday after Christmas Day" (Book of Common Prayer, page 213) followed by some singing of Christmas carols, many noted below.

> Almighty God, you have poured upon us the new light of your incarnate Word: Grant that this light, enkindled in our hearts, may shine forth in our lives; through Jesus Christ our Lord, who lives and reigns with you, in the unity of the Holy Spirit, one God, now and forever. *Amen.*

A selection of Christmas carols

- O Little Town of Bethlehem
- O Come, All Ye Faithful
- Hark! The Herald Angels Sing
- It Came Upon the Midnight Clear
- Angels We Have Heard on High
- Go Tell It on the Mountain
- Joy to the World!
- Away in a Manger
- The First Noel
- Silent Night
- What Child Is This
- People Look East
- Rise Up, Shepherd, and Follow

CRAFTS
Name Banners

In scripture, Jesus is given many names. We may see these symbols at our churches and even on bumper stickers, but do we know what they mean or where they come from? This activity allows for some creativity while learning about the meanings and origins of names associated with Jesus from birth to resurrection.

Materials

- 36 dowels, ½" thick (2 for each banner)
- 30" x 60" rectangle of burlap (1 for each banner)
- fabric glue
- felt or other fabric in assorted colors
- trimmings, braid, rick-rack, piping, cording, sequins, beads, etc.
- scissors
- fabric markers
- twine
- Bibles and prayer books
- paper
- pens/pencils
- copies of a handout with symbols and descriptions of Jesus, 1 per group (also download at *www.churchpublishing.org /faithfulcelebrations3*)

Directions

1. Divide the participants into groups of 5–10. Invite each group to make a name banner for Jesus, using one or several symbols to represent different names of Jesus.

2. Provide each group with a copy of the handout with traditional symbols for the names of Jesus. Encourage them to brainstorm other possibilities, looking at the Bible and prayer books for ideas to create their own symbols.

3. When each group has compiled a list of new and traditional names, ask them to cut letters and symbols from fabric to glue onto the burlap. Use the markers, braid, piping, sequins, etc., to embellish the letters and symbols.

4. Glue each 30" edge of burlap around a dowel. Ask participants to glue the names to the banners. Fasten twine to the ends of the top dowels to hang the banners.

Traditional Symbols for the Names of Jesus

Chi Rho
(first two letters of Greek spelling of Christ)

Alpha and Omega
Revelation 1:8
and 22:13

INRI
Latin inscription on cross of Calvary (John 19:19) meaning "Jesus of Nazareth, King of the Jews"

Crown of Life
Psalm 24:7-10
Revelation 11:15

Chi Rho with Anchor
(a symbol of hope)
Titus 2:13

IHS
(monogram derived from first three letters in Greek spelling of "Jesus")
Matthew 1:21

Ichthus
(Greek letters spell fish and make a rebus "Jesus Christ, God's Son, Savior")

**Agnus Dei
Lamb of God with
Banner of Victory**
Revelation 5:12-14

Rising Sun
Malachi 4:2

Bright and Morning Star
Revelation 22:16

Star of David
Numbers 24:17
Revelation 22:16

Manger with Chi Rho
Luke 2:11-12

Seeing Jesus, Knowing God

At Christmas, we celebrate the incarnation of Christ, a short period in history when God became human and walked on earth. This activity challenges participants to think about how we see Christ on earth today, even though he doesn't physically walk among us.

Materials

- construction paper
- old magazines
- scissors
- glue
- markers

Directions

1. Begin by discussing the following questions:
   - How do you perceive Jesus in the gospels?
   - What qualities describe Jesus?
   - What roles describe Jesus?
   - What evidence do we have from scripture that these qualities and roles describe God?
   - What evidence do we have from experience that these qualities and roles describe God?
   - How do we experience Jesus in the world today?

2. Invite participants to make a collage that represents how they experience Jesus in the world today by cutting pictures and words from magazines and gluing them onto construction paper. They might also include images that reflect the different names and roles of Christ: *alpha and omega, healer, teacher,* and so on.

3. Once the collages are completed, give each person an opportunity to describe his/her collage to the group.

No one has ever seen God. It is God the only Son, who is close to the Father's heart, who has made him known. —John 1:18

Shoe Box Crèches

Materials

- modeling clay or play dough
- shoe boxes
- cardboard
- scissors
- glue
- pencils, pens, or other styluses for adding detail to clay
- dried pine needles, excelsior (wood shavings used for packing material), or shredded paper

Directions

1. Show the participants how to make figures—of Mary, Joseph, the baby, or the animals—by pulling appendages out of a single piece of clay. (Some people may want to make shepherds and an angel, too.)
2. Invite each child to make a figure from the nativity story, using a pencil, pen, or stylus to add details such as facial features and clothing textures.
3. Use a shoe box as a stable for each crèche. Mangers and troughs may be cut from cardboard. Pine needles can be used for straw on the floor.
4. Display completed crèches somewhere in your gathering area or the church for others to enjoy through the Christmas season.

Holy Family Mural

Groups can work together to create scenes from the life of the Holy Family to make one large mural.

Materials

- Bibles
- butcher paper or newsprint

- tape
- markers/crayons/colored pencils

Directions

1. Divide the participants into five groups.
2. Tape a long sheet (at least 15 feet) of butcher paper to a wall or place on the floor.
3. Assign one of the following short Bible passages about the Holy Family to each group:
   - Matthew 1:18–24
   - Matthew 2:13–15, 19–23
   - Luke 2:15–21
   - Luke 2:22–40
   - Luke 2:41–51
4. Ask each group to read the passage and create a design for its assigned scene. Have each group draw its scene on a section of the butcher paper so the scenes are presented chronologically.
5. Display the mural someplace throughout the Christmas season.

STORYTELLING AND BIBLE STUDY

A Child is Born

Gather the youngest children around and read them this vibrant version of the Christmas story. Afterwards, lead them in a discussion of what they like most about the story and what they think it tells us about God. Remember that there are no right or wrong responses.

Emmanuel, God with Us

God called the angels together and they crowded about, leaning forward with excitement to hear the news.

God spoke: "This day my Son, Jesus, has been born in Bethlehem. He will show all people how deeply I love them. They will learn from him what it is like to be with me. They will even call him Emmanuel—God with us.

"Go now, angels! Not one, not two, not three of you, but all of you! Go and tell the good news. Tell the news to the shepherds taking care of their sheep in fields near Bethlehem. Tell the news to kings who live far away."

Off the angels flew to sing a new song of good news: "A child is born. His name is Jesus and he is God's Son. Glory to God in the highest, and peace to God's people on earth."

As the angels sang, a new star appeared in the sky. It came to rest right over the stable in Bethlehem where Jesus, Mary, and Joseph were staying.

The shepherds who were taking care of their sheep in the fields nearby were amazed and frightened at the brightness of the star. But then they saw an angel. Can you imagine how they trembled?

The angel said to them, "Don't be afraid, for I bring you good news of great joy. To you this very day in Bethlehem, a Child—a Savior—has been born. He is Christ the Lord. You will know this Child when you find a newborn Baby wrapped in strips of cloth and lying in a manger."

Suddenly the shepherds saw not just one angel, but thousands of angels, all the host of heaven. The angels were singing, "Glory to God in the highest and peace to God's people on earth."

When the angels left, the shepherds said to one another, "Let's go into Bethlehem right now and look for this Baby. Just imagine, angels came to tell us! Why, we may be the first to know! Us! Just simple shepherds. Let's run! Hurry! See the bright star? It hangs there low in the sky. Follow it. Hurry! Hurry!"

Away the shepherds ran, as fast as they could go. They found the stable where Mary and Joseph were. They found Jesus lying in a manger, wrapped in swaddling clothes, just as the angel had told them. This was the Baby. This was the Savior!

"We came to see the Baby," the shepherds said.

"His name is Jesus," Joseph whispered to the shepherds.

"How did you know about him?" Mary asked.

"How did you know to look here?" Joseph asked.

The shepherds told Mary and Joseph all they had heard and seen, about the sky full of angels and the new, bright star. One of the shepherds said to Joseph, "The angels said 'to you a child has been born.' What can that mean? Could it mean that this Baby, this Savior, came to show you and me God's love?"

The shepherd smiled and looked shyly at Joseph. "You know," he said, "if Jesus were born into my family, this is just the kind of place he would be born. My children came into the world on our farm, and there were more animals around than people! Why, Jesus even looks a lot like my youngest did. But there's something special about this child, isn't there?"

Joseph smiled and placed his hand on the shepherd's shoulder. "Yes," Joseph said, "there is. This Baby is God's Son. There is more to his birth than even his mother and I understand. But rejoice and celebrate with us, because this child will save his people."

Joseph, Mary, and the shepherds smiled at the Baby sleeping in the manger. Their hearts and voices sang grateful songs of praise to God. The angels in heaven rejoiced because God's plan was being carried out in this simple place with these simple people.

"Hallelujah! To all of us a Child is born! Hallelujah! Hallelujah!"

Crèche Sharing

Invite participants to bring and display their crèches. During the Celebration, invite individuals to share stories about their crèches with the gathered group, such as the history of the crèche and traditions that they observe. If your church has a traditional crèche with an interesting story, invite a long-standing member or leader also to share that story with the group.

You might do this at the beginning of your Celebration as participants arrive. This could be a great icebreaker or a conversation-starter during snack time.

Materials

- family and personal crèches (*Note:* In advance, invite willing individuals, couples, and families to bring their crèches to the Celebration.)
- tables
- *optional*: congregation's crèche

Light of the World Discussion

Materials

- Bibles (a variety of translations might offer more insights)

Directions

1. Distribute Bibles and invite someone to read John 1:1–5, 10–14 aloud to the group.
2. If you are using more than one translation, read those aloud also.
3. Discussion questions:
   - In what ways do you see darkness in our world today?
   - How does that darkness not see, recognize, or understand the light of Jesus? What are the barriers that keep the light of Jesus from being seen?
   - What difference would understanding the light of Christ make in that area of darkness?
   - How can Christians, as bearers of the light, take that light to areas of darkness in our world?

DRAMA

On-the-Spot Pageant

Hold an impromptu Christmas pageant by inviting participants to act out with silent movements the Christmas story, as it is read.

Materials

- books or hymnals with Christmas carols
- Bibles
- copies of The Christmas Story in Four Parts (found on pages 118–119 or download at *www.churchpublishing.org/faithful celebrations3*)
- *optional:* makeshift costumes and props

Directions

1. Ask one group of participants to be the chorus; give them song books and a list of the carols to be practiced.
2. Choose one or more narrators who will be the only speaking parts.
3. Ask the other participants to choose parts from this list and have them practice their movements.

    - Mary
    - Joseph
    - animals in manger
    - shepherds
    - angels

The Christmas Story in Four Parts

Read: Luke 2:1–4

At that time Emperor Augustus ordered a census to be taken throughout the Roman Empire. When this first census took place, Quirinius was the governor of Syria. Everyone, then, went to register himself, each to his own hometown. Joseph went from the town of Nazareth in Galilee to the town of Bethlehem in Judea, the birthplace of King David. Joseph went there because he was a descendant of David.

Sing: "O, Little Town of Bethlehem"

Read: Luke 2:5–7

He went to register with Mary, who was promised in marriage to him. She was pregnant, and while they were in Bethlehem, the time came for her to have her baby. She gave birth to her first son, wrapped him in cloths and laid him in a manger—there was no room for them to stay in the inn.

Sing: "Silent Night, Holy Night"

Read: Luke 2:8–14

There were some shepherds in that part of the country who were spending the night in the fields, taking care of their flocks. An angel of the Lord appeared to them, and the glory of the Lord shone over them. They were terribly afraid, but the angel said to them, "Don't be afraid! I am here with good news for you, which will bring great joy to all the people. This very day in David's town your Savior was born—Christ the Lord! And this is what will prove it to you: you will find a baby wrapped in cloths and lying in a manger." Suddenly a great army of heaven's angels appeared with the angel, singing praises to God: "Glory to God in the highest heaven, and peace on earth to those with whom he is pleased!"

Sing: "Go, Tell It On the Mountain"

Read: Luke 2:15–20

When the angels went away from them back into heaven, the shepherds said to one another, "Let's go to Bethlehem and see this thing that has happened, which the Lord has told us." So they hurried off and found Mary and Joseph and saw the baby lying in the manger. When the shepherds saw him, they told them what the angel had said about the child. All who heard it were amazed at what the shepherds said. Mary remembered all these things and thought deeply about them. The shepherds went back, singing praises to God for all they had heard and seen; it had been just as the angel had told them.

Sing: "O Come, All Ye Faithful"

GAMES

What's Missing?

This game can be simplified for the youngest participants by limiting the number of figures to three or four. Ways to increase the game's difficulty include:

- using more items
- rearranging the items before removing one
- removing more than one item
- rearranging the items without removing any

Materials

- crèche with figures

Directions

1. Ask participants to close their eyes.
2. Remove one figure from the crèche.
3. Ask participants to open their eyes and guess which figure is missing. Return the missing figure to the crèche; whoever guesses correctly gets to remove the next figure.

Put the Star on the Tree

Here is a Christmas version of "Pin the Tail on the Donkey."

Materials

- butcher paper or newsprint
- markers
- masking tape
- scissors
- 3" stars cut from yellow construction paper
- blindfold

Directions

1. Use the markers to draw a Christmas tree, approximately three feet high, on the butcher paper.

2. Tape the tree to a wall of the room.

3. Put a loop of masking tape on the back of each star. Invite everyone to play "Put the Star on the Tree."

4. Blindfold one player at a time and give the player a star. Turn the player around in a slow circle twice then give them a gentle push in the right direction.

5. Ask the player to walk to the wall and touch it. When the player touches the wall, he or she must stick the star on the exact spot touched. Let the player remove the blindfold, and write his or her name on the star.

6. Repeat until everyone has had a turn. The winner is the one to stick a star closest to the top of the tree.

RECIPES

Wassail Punch

All ages will enjoy making this traditional Christmas beverage. You might want to increase the amounts and have the children serve this to the entire group.

Ingredients

- 1 gallon apple cider
- 2 cinnamon sticks
- 1 whole nutmeg
- 5–6 whole cloves

Supplies

- stainless steel or enameled pot, at least 6 quart capacity

Directions

1. Put all the ingredients in a pot.
2. Bring to a simmer, but do not boil.
3. Simmer for 30 minutes. Serve warm.

Christmas Stollen

Christmas isn't complete without the fruitcake, and this Christstollen is a holiday staple in Germany—it's similar to the Dutch Kerststol and the Italian panettone.

Ingredients

Stollen:

- ¾ cup milk
- ½ cup water
- ½ cup (1 stick) butter
- 4¼ cups bread flour (not self-rising)

- ½ cup granulated sugar
- 2 teaspoons salt
- 2 envelopes active dry yeast
- 1 egg
- ¾ cup candied fruit
- ¾ cup nuts, such as almonds, pecans, and/or walnuts, chopped
- ½ cup raisins
- 1 teaspoon grated lemon rind
- 1 teaspoon grated orange rind
- ¾ teaspoon ground mace

Topping:
- 2 tablespoons butter, melted
- ¼ cup granulated sugar
- 3 tablespoons confectioners' sugar

Directions
Stollen:

1. Heat milk, water, and butter in small saucepan until 120° on instant-read thermometer.
2. Whisk 1¼ cups flour, the sugar, salt and yeast in large bowl. Add warm milk mixture; beat on medium 2 minutes. Add egg and 1 cup flour; beat on high 2 minutes. Stir in remaining flour until batter is stiff. Transfer to greased bowl; turn to coat. Cover with plastic; let rise in warm place until doubled, 1½ hours.
3. Combine candied fruit, nuts, raisins, rinds, and mace in bowl. Knead fruit mixture into dough.
4. Divide dough into thirds. On surface, roll third into oval, 10 x 8 inches. Fold in half lengthwise; curve each end slightly. Transfer each to greased baking sheet. Cover with plastic wrap; let rise in warm place until doubled, 1 to 1½ hours. Repeat with remaining dough.

5. Bake at 350°for 35 minutes or until bottom of stollen sounds hollow when lightly tapped. Let cool on rack.

Topping:

1. Brush loaves with melted butter.
2. Sprinkle with granulated sugar.
3. Dust tops with the confectioners' sugar.

WORSHIP

Closing Prayer

Choose one or both of the following options for your closing prayer:

> Thank you, God, for being a God of surprise! The world waited for a King—and you sent a baby. Thank you for the joyful surprises you send us. Help us to share your wonderful surprises with those who don't yet know you. *Amen.*

Lower the lights in the room and light a candle. Close with a few quiet moments for participants to choose their favorite name for Jesus and let each participant say his or her chosen name. Thank God for sending our Savior to be light in the darkness.

Chapter 6

EPIPHANY

INTRODUCTION

The word *Epiphany* means manifestation. The readings for Epiphany manifest, or reveal, the person and nature of Jesus.

The feast of Epiphany is celebrated on January 6, a date chosen in ancient times to counteract a pagan festival in Egypt that marked the winter solstice. The pagan festival used themes of light, water, and wine. Making use of these same elements, the Eastern Church celebrates the revelation of Jesus Christ at his birth, marked by the light of the Nativity star; at his baptism in water; and at Cana, where he changed water to wine.

The Western Church, which had begun to celebrate Christmas on December 25 in opposition to a pagan winter solstice in Rome, appropriated some, but not all, of the Eastern significance of Epiphany. In the West, celebration of Epiphany emphasized the visit of the magi, guided by the Nativity star. This event came to be interpreted as the revelation of Jesus Christ to the Gentiles.

Remembering the Magi

Scripture does not describe the number or race or mode of travel of the magi. The biblical emphasis is on the magi's three gifts: gold, frankincense, and myrrh. These gifts reveal the royal, divine, and sacrificial nature of the infant Jesus.

Many customs exist in European countries that give the day far more significance than in our own culture. Some countries use this day, rather than Christmas Day, as the time to exchange gifts. Other countries observe the day with "Star Carols" sung by a procession of singers, dressed as magi and carrying stars.

The Baptism of Jesus

The Baptism of Jesus, observed on the first Sunday after Epiphany, is an important feast of the season. At his baptism, Jesus is revealed as the Son of God and sealed by God's Holy Spirit. After this feast, the Sundays of Ordinary Time, between Epiphany and Lent, reveal Jesus enacting his baptismal ministry of preaching, teaching, and healing.

Our own baptisms share in this manifestation or revelation. At baptism, each of us stood revealed as God's own child, sealed with the Holy Spirit, and called to ministry and mission.

As we come to the end of the Christmas season, let us look with joy to our Savior, revealed by the star that shone at his birth, by the waters of his baptism, and by the power of his ministry. See, the Lord goes forth to teach, to preach, and to heal. Let us look—and then follow.

WORSHIP

Opening Prayer

The gospel for Epiphany is from Matthew 2:1–12. Proclaim this gospel at the beginning of your Celebration:

> Jesus was born in the town of Bethlehem in Judea, during the time when Herod was king. Soon afterward, some men who studied the stars came from the East to Jerusalem and asked, "Where is the baby born to be the king of the Jews? We saw his star when it came up in the east, and we have come to worship him."
>
> When King Herod heard about this, he was very upset, and so was everyone else in Jerusalem. He called together all the chief priests and the teachers of the Law and asked them, "Where will the Messiah be born?"
>
> "In the town of Bethlehem in Judea," they answered. "For this is what the prophet wrote:
>
>> Bethlehem in the land of Judah,
>> you are by no means the least of the leading cities of Judah;
>> for from you will come a leader
>> who will guide my people Israel."
>
> So Herod called the visitors from the East to a secret meeting and found out from them the exact time the star had appeared. Then he sent them to Bethlehem with these instructions: "Go and make a careful search for the child; and when you find him, let me know, so that I too may go and worship him."
>
> And so they left, and on their way they saw the same star they had seen in the East. When they saw it, how happy they were, what joy was theirs! It went ahead of them until it stopped over the place where the child was. They went into the house, and when they saw the child with his mother Mary, they knelt down and worshiped him. They brought

out their gifts of gold, frankincense, and myrrh, and presented them to him.

Then they returned to their country by another road, since God had warned them in a dream not to go back to Herod.

The Blessing of the Home

From the time of the Middle Ages it has been a tradition that on the feast of the Epiphany we pray for God's blessing on our dwelling places, marking the entrance to our homes with chalk. Chalk is used as a tangible reminder of the dust of the earth from which we are all made.

We mark the main door of our home with the initials of the magi and the numerals of the new year. The initials remind us of the names of the magi—Caspar, Melchior, and Balthasar—and also stand for the Latin motto: *Christus mansionem benedicat*, "May Christ bless this house." We connect the initials and the numerals with crosses as a sign that we have invited God's presence and blessing into our homes.

If your Celebration is taking place in a home, use this liturgy as part of your event. If being held at your church, gather everyone to bless the chalk. Then invite everyone to take the chalk home to bless their homes after your gathering.

The Blessing of the Chalk

Participants gather around a basket containing pieces of ordinary white or colored chalk.

Materials

- chalk (1 per family)
- basket
- copies of "The Blessing of the Home" (1 per family, couple or individual, see p. 130) (download at *www.churchpublishing.org /faithfulcelebrations3*)

The Blessing

Leader: God dwells in you.

Participants: And also with you.

Leader: Let us pray. Bless, O Lord, this chalk that it may be a sign of your blessing upon the homes of your people. We pray that, like wise men and women of old, we may serve him as our only King, worship him as the one true God, and honor him with lives of sacrifice and praise, who lives and reigns with you and the Holy Spirit, one God, for ever and ever. *Amen.*

The Blessing of the Home

The blessing of the house begins with all members of the household at the entrance of the home. A member of the family leads the blessing.

Leader: Peace be to this house.

Participants: And to all who enter here.

The Leader speaks the following while marking the doorway with the chalk as indicated:

Leader: Wise ones came to honor the Savior and offer him gifts.

C   Caspar,

M   Melchior,

B   and Balthasar followed the star of God's Son who became human

two thousand and [*insert current year*] years ago.

++ May Christ bless our home and all who join us here,

++ and remain with us throughout the new year. *Amen.*

20 + C + M + B + 19 (or current year)

All: May this Epiphany blessing be a reminder of Christ's presence among us and a symbol of God's love and care as we share the blessings and burdens of our daily lives.

CRAFTS

Epiphany Crowns

Invite participants to wear crowns as they eat Three Kings Cake (page 146) or sing Star Carols (page 139).

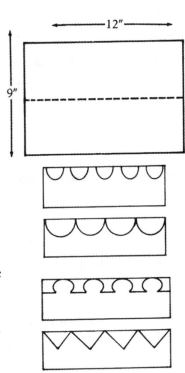

Materials

- 9" x 12" construction paper in assorted colors
- scissors
- crayons and markers
- glitter
- gummed stars
- glue
- clear tape or stapler

Directions

1. Demonstrate how to make simple construction-paper crowns by cutting a 9" x 12" rectangle of construction paper in half lengthwise. Cut the top edges into various shapes.

2. Decorate the crowns while flat, using materials such as glitter, crayons, markers, construction paper shapes, gummed stars, etc.

3. Glue, tape, or staple the two ends of each crown together, being careful to check the fit first. (You will need two identical strips taped together to make a large enough crown.)

Epiphany Star

Invite participants to make an Epiphany Star to symbolize the mission and ministry of Jesus. Some of the stories suggested here are traditional stories associated with the feast of Epiphany or the

Baptism of the Lord. Others are drawn from the weeks of Ordinary Time preceding Lent. Plan to hang the star in a public part of your church building or home.

Materials

- Bibles
- scissors
- 4' square of yellow felt
- 6' square of white cloth for background
- glue
- 9" x 12" felt rectangles
- felt scraps
- trimmings, sequins, beads, rick-rack, etc.
- *optional:* straight pins

Directions

1. Ask one participant to cut the 4' x 4' yellow square into two triangles. (Cut a diagonal line across the square to make the two triangles.) Overlap the triangles to make a six-pointed star. Glue the star onto the white background.

2. Divide the other participants into six groups. Ask each group to make one felt collage symbol to represent one of these stories listed below.

Visit of the Magi
reading: Matthew 2:1–12
symbol: star or crown

Call of the Fishermen
reading: Luke 5:1–11
symbol: fish

Baptism of Jesus
reading: Mark 1:9–11
symbol: shell or dove

Jesus the Teacher
reading: Luke 8:16–21
symbol: lamp

Wedding at Cana
reading: John 2:1–11
symbol: water jar or wine cup

Jesus the Healer
reading: Mark 1:29–34
symbol: hands or flask of oil

3. Encourage each group to read and discuss its story. You may wish to have each group devise its own symbol, in order to encourage more discussion.

4. Have each group cut a 9" round from a 9" x 12" rectangle of felt and then construct its symbol, using this felt round for a background. Trim the symbols with shapes cut from felt scraps, beads, rick-rack, etc.

5. Participants place the finished symbols on the Epiphany Star. Use glue or straight pins, if necessary, to secure the symbols.

STORYTELLING AND BIBLE STUDY

Storytelling Round

Tell the story of the birth of Jesus and the visit of the magi by holding a Story Round.

Materials

- star-shaped Christmas tree ornament *or* star cut from cardboard and covered with gold or silver foil

Directions

1. Ask participants to sit in a circle. Begin the story with a sentence or two, such as:

   At that time, the emperor demanded that everyone go to his hometown to be counted so that the emperor could collect tax money from all of his people. Joseph and Mary traveled to Joseph's home city of Bethlehem, to be counted. . . .

2. Hand the star to the next person in the circle, who continues the story by adding a sentence.

3. Then that person passes the star to the next person in the circle, who continues the story and hands on the star.

4. Continue around the circle until the whole story has been told.

Gifts for Jesus

Materials

- Bible or copy of *The Visit of the Kings* (p. 135)
- paper
- crayons, colored pencils, or markers
- tape

Directions

1. Read *The Visit of the Kings* (below) or read the story from Matthew 2:1–12. Ask the following questions:

   - How did the magi try to find Jesus?
   - How do we try to find Jesus?
   - What gifts did the magi bring?
   - What gifts can we bring?

2. Encourage participants to express respect for every answer. For example, if a child says "a skateboard" in answer to the last question, look the child directly in the eyes as you say, "You'd like to give Jesus a skateboard. I think Jesus would have fun playing with that!"

3. When participants have had a chance to express their ideas, ask everyone to write or draw presents to give to Jesus. If participants choose, invite everyone to share their "gifts for Jesus."

The Visit of the Kings

When Jesus is born in Bethlehem, a star shines in the sky right over the stable. Three kings in faraway lands see that new star. They know it means that something very special has happened. So they set out on their camels to follow the star. They follow the star for many days and many miles.

When the three kings arrive in Jerusalem, they stop to talk to the king of that land. His name is Herod. He is not a very good king at all. In fact, he is mean and wicked. Herod asks, "What are you doing in my country?"

The kings tell him, "We are here to worship a newborn king. We have seen his star in the sky."

Herod is not happy when he hears that a new king is born. He asks the three wise men to come back to him after they find the new king. He says he wants to worship the newborn king, too. (But he is not telling the truth!)

The star moves across the sky and the three kings follow it. The star leads them on to Bethlehem and stops at the place where Jesus and Mary and Joseph live. The three kings go to the door and knock. (How do you think Mary and Joseph feel when they see three kings standing at their door?)

The kings have special gifts for Jesus. They carry the gifts in and lay them down by Baby Jesus. The gifts are gold, sweet smelling incense, and myrrh, used as perfume or medicine.

The kings "ooh" and "ahh" at the beautiful baby. They smile and hold out their fingers for Jesus to squeeze. They laugh and tickle the baby, and make him smile and laugh. (Have you ever seen people do this to babies?)

The kings say goodbye to the little family and start their long journey home. They set up camp that night not far from Bethlehem. They eat supper and fall fast asleep.

That night in a dream God talks to the three kings. He says, "Do not go back and tell wicked King Herod about Jesus. Go home another way. Herod is evil and he wants to hurt Jesus!"

The next morning the kings start home by a road that leads far, far away from King Herod's palace. They sing and laugh and give thanks to God for his gift of Jesus to the world.

The Baptism of Jesus

The Feast of the Baptism of Jesus is celebrated on the Sunday after January 6. The season of Epiphany, which lasts until Lent begins, is about Jesus' ministry and call to bring the Good News to others. It is a time to remember our own baptisms and recall our mission as Christians.

Materials

- Bibles
- paper
- pens or pencils

Directions

1. Invite participants to look up the four Bible passages given below, spending 5 minutes noting the differences and similarities between them.

2. Discuss:
   - How are these passages similar?
   - How do these passages differ?
   - What would you choose as the most important emphasis of each passage? How could we outline the events of Jesus' baptism?
   - Do these events have counterparts in our rites of baptism today?
   - Do these events have counterparts in our daily lives as Christians?

3. If your group is large, divide everyone into small groups to discuss these questions:
   - How would you define the mission of Jesus after his baptism?
   - How would you define the mission of baptized Christians?
   - How does this understanding of mission affect your daily life?

The Baptism of Jesus in the Four Gospels

Matthew 3:13–17

Then Jesus came from Galilee to John at the Jordan, to be baptized by him. John would have prevented him, saying, "I need to be baptized by you, and do you come to me?" But Jesus answered him, "Let it be so now; for it is proper for us in this way to fulfill all righteousness." Then he consented. And when Jesus had been baptized, just as he came up from the water, suddenly the heavens were opened to him and he saw the Spirit of God descending like a dove and alighting on him. And a voice from heaven said, "This is my Son, the Beloved, with whom I am pleased."

Mark 1:9–11

In those days Jesus came from Nazareth of Galilee, and was baptized by John in the Jordan. And just as he was coming up out of the water, he saw the heavens torn apart and the Spirit descending like a dove upon him. And a voice came from heaven, "You are my Son, the Beloved; with you I am well pleased."

Luke 3:21–22

Now when all the people were baptized, and when Jesus also had been baptized and was praying, the heaven was opened, and the Holy Spirit descended upon him in bodily form like a dove. And a voice came from heaven, "You are my Son, the Beloved; with you I am pleased."

John 1:29–34

The next day he saw Jesus coming toward him and declared, "Here is the Lamb of God who takes away the sin of the world! This is he of whom I said, 'After me comes a man, ranks ahead of me because he was before me.' I myself did not know him; but I came baptizing with water for this reason, that he might be revealed to Israel." And John testified, "I saw the Spirit descending from heaven like a dove, and it remained on him. I myself did not know him, but the one who who sent me to baptize with water said to me, 'He on whom you see the Spirit descend and remain is the one who baptizes with the Holy Spirit.' And I myself have seen and have testified that this is the Son of God."

MUSIC

Star Carol Procession

At one time, people in European countries watched Epiphany plays performed by traveling groups of players. A vestige of this custom is retained in the Star Carol procession, in which carolers go from place to place singing hymns appropriate to the season. The carolers carry poles topped by stars—to recall the star of Bethlehem—and sometimes dress in costumes—to represent the magi and their entourage.

Your Epiphany celebration might include a Star Carol procession in your neighborhood. First, make some stars. Then choose some carols to sing.

Materials

- poles, dowels, or sticks
- cardboard
- yellow construction paper or metallic foil/gift wrap
- glue
- scissors or a mat knife (for older children and adult use only)
- staple gun (for older children and adult use only)
- *optional:* glitter, sequins, beads, etc.; makeshift costumes; songbooks

Directions

1. Provide poles, sticks, or dowels for the star poles.
2. Participants glue yellow construction paper over cardboard, then cut out stars.
3. A mat knife will be easier to use than scissors, but keep the knife away from small children.
4. Decorate the stars with glitter, sequins, streamers, etc., and use a staple gun to attach the stars to the poles.

Songs appropriate for Epiphany include:

- We Three Kings
- Go Tell It on the Mountain
- What Child Is This
- Brightest and Best
- What Star Is This?

DRAMA

Mock TV Reports

Materials

- Bibles

Directions

1. Divide the participants into three groups to prepare a mock TV report on the Baptism of our Lord.

2. Pass out Bibles to the participants, and ask them to use Matthew 3:13–17 (see page 137) as the basis of the TV special.

3. Remind all the groups of the "five w's" of good reporting: *Who? What? Where? When?* and *Why?*

4. Allow 10–15 minutes for planning, then reconvene and allow groups to present their interviews.

   Group 1: Ask one member of the group to play the part of John the Baptist. Ask the other members to play reporters. Prepare questions and answers.

   Group 2: Ask several members of the group to play the parts of bystanders. Ask the other members to play reporters. Prepare questions and answers.

   Group 3: Ask one member of the group to play the part of Jesus. Ask the other members to play reporters. Prepare questions and answers.

GAME

King's Journey

This game, similar to "Duck, Duck, Goose," is especially suitable for young children.

Materials

- road map

Directions

1. Ask participants to sit in a circle.
2. Choose one participant to be *It* and give him/her a folded road map. The person who is *It* walks around the outside of the circle as the group chants this rhyme:

   We've followed the star a long, long way
   We've followed the star a long, long way
   We've followed the star a long, long way
   How many miles will we travel today?

3. As the group says the word *today*, *It* drops the road map in the lap of the nearest player, and runs around the circle, trying to get to that player's place before the player with the road map tags *It*.
4. If *It* gets to the place, the participant with the road map becomes *It*, and the game continues.
5. If *It* gets tagged, the same player continues to be *It*.

FAITH IN ACTION

Baptismal Calendars

This activity gives a tangible way for participants to think how they might live out their baptismal promises throughout the season of Epiphany.

Materials

- whiteboard, poster board, or newsprint
- markers
- copies of a blank calendar for as many weeks as are needed for the Sundays between the Baptism of the Lord and Lent, 1 per participant (download at *www.churchpublishing.org /faithfulcelebrations3*)
- pens or pencils
- *optional:* 9" x 12" drawing paper; crayons or markers; scissors; glue or glue sticks

Directions

1. Invite participants to brainstorm ideas for a baptismal mission calendar. Think of activities that carry out our baptismal mission, and record all ideas on whiteboard, poster board, or newsprint.

2. Suggestions you may wish to add include:
   - visit someone lonely today
   - write a friendly note to another Christian today
   - write a friendly note to a non-Christian today
   - borrow some children's books from the library, and offer to read at the hospital today
   - pray for world peace, and for troubled areas particularly

3. When the group has generated enough ideas, have each participant or family make a baptismal calendar to take home.

4. Ask each participant to choose favorite activities, then write these on a blank calendar.

SUNDAY	MONDAY	TUESDAY	WEDNESDAY	THURSDAY	FRIDAY	SATURDAY

Note: The number of weeks in Epiphany changes from year to year. Instead of using a template of a calendar, there is an option to create your own calendar of squares based on the weeks of Epiphany in the current year.

Epiphany Resolutions

The beginning of the new year is a good time to make Epiphany resolutions and promises.

Materials

- paper
- pens or pencils
- envelopes
- stamps

Directions

1. Invite participants to quietly determine how they could live Jesus' message of peace and justice in their own homes, in their neighborhoods, and in the world.

2. Ask them to write down these "resolutions," sealing them in self-addressed stamped envelopes.

3. Leaders can hold the resolutions for a few weeks or months before mailing them back to the owners as reminders of their commitments.

RECIPES

Three Kings Cake

The Three Kings Cake is a European tradition. The cake—usually a flat circle, more like a cookie than a cake—hides a bean or two, a doll, or a clutch of tiny fortunes. The significance of the hidden fortune varies. A hidden dime might signify wealth in the coming year. The finders of two dry beans might become king and queen of the Epiphany party. In New Orleans, the finder of a hidden black bean or baby must give a party for all the other guests. Invite participants to make a traditional Kings Cake at home and bring it to the celebration.

Ingredients

- ½ cup blanched almonds
- 1 cup sugar
- 6 tablespoons soft butter (save the wrapper)
- 1 teaspoon vanilla or almond extract
- 2 eggs, lightly beaten
- 2 tablespoons raisins or currants
- 2¼ cups flour
- 1½ teaspoons baking powder

Supplies

- blender or food processor
- bowl
- spoon
- cookie sheet
- forks
- *optional:* beans, dimes, small plastic baby

Directions

1. Grind the almonds with ¼ cup sugar in a food processor or blender.

2. Use a fork to mix the butter and sugar together in a bowl. Mix until the butter and sugar are thoroughly blended. Beat in the eggs (saving a tablespoon of egg to glaze the top) and the extract.

3. Sift together the flour and baking powder into the egg mixture. Stir in the sugar-almond mix, the raisins or currants, and any fortunes—such as beans—desired.

4. Turn the dough onto a greased cookie sheet. (Use the paper wrapping from the butter to grease the sheet.) Pat the dough flat into a ½" thick circle.

5. Spread the reserved beaten egg on the top of the cake.

6. Bake at 350° for 20 minutes.

Serves 12 people.

Zimtsterne—Cinnamon Stars

The dough can be made ahead of time if you want to actually make these cookies during your Celebration.

Ingredients

- ¼ cup margarine or butter
- ¼ cup honey
- ¼ cup sugar
- 2 large eggs
- 3 cups flour
- 2 teaspoon baking powder
- ½ teaspoon baking soda
- 1 teaspoon ground cinnamon
- ½ teaspoon ground nutmeg
- ¼ teaspoon ground cloves
- ½ cup unsweetened apple juice
- *optional:* 1 tablespoon Kirschwasser or clear cherry juice
- star pattern cookie cutter

Directions

1. Cream the margarine, honey, sugar, and eggs together in a bowl until smooth and fluffy. Add the remaining ingredients and mix well.
2. Divide the dough into three equal parts and roll each one into a circle about ½ inch thick.
3. Wrap each in plastic wrap and refrigerate overnight.
4. Remove the dough from the refrigerator and roll out on a lightly floured surface to about ⅛-inch thickness.
5. Cut cookies out with the star cookie cutter and place on a lightly greased baking sheet.
6. Bake in the 375° oven for 8–10 minutes or until lightly browned.

Makes 5 dozen.

Pfeffernusse

The dough for this traditional holiday cookie must be prepared a day ahead and allowed to chill.

Ingredients

- ¼ cup corn syrup or molasses
- 1¼ cups honey
- ¼ cup sweet unsalted butter, cut into pieces
- 4 cups all purpose flour
- *optional:* 2 tablespoons unsweetened cocoa powder
- 1 teaspoon baking soda
- ½ teaspoon ground cardamom
- ¼ teaspoon freshly grated nutmeg
- ¼ teaspoon ground allspice
- ¼ teaspoon ground cloves
- ¼ teaspoon freshly ground black pepper

- ⅛ teaspoon salt
- 1 large egg
- ¼ teaspoon pure anise extract
- powdered sugar

Directions

1. Combine corn syrup/molasses, honey and butter in a small sauce pan and cook over low heat, being careful to not bring mixture to a boil. When thoroughly melted remove from heat and put aside to cool.
2. When syrup mixture has cooled, beat egg and add to syrup. Add anise and beat well.
3. In a separate bowl, sift together flour, salt, baking soda, spices, and cocoa powder.
4. Slowly add dry ingredients into the wet ingredients using a large spoon. When done mixture should form a stiff dough.
5. Chill overnight.
6. Lightly grease and flour a cookie sheet.
7. Using approximately 1 tablespoon of dough for each cookie, roll the dough into balls between the palms of your hands and place on prepared cookie sheets.
8. Bake for 9–12 minutes in preheated over of 375° until golden. If you use the cocoa, bake a test batch of 3–4 cookies as the dark coloring may make it difficult to tell when cookies are done.
9. Remove from oven. Let cool.

Makes 5 dozen.

Lamb's Wool Punch

This old English and Irish punch, which dates from the Middle Ages, probably gets its name from the wooly appearance of the flesh of the roasted apples floating in the cider.

Ingredients

- 6 baking apples, cored
- 2 tablespoons to ½ cup brown sugar
- 2 quarts sweet cider, hard cider, or ale, or a mixture of cider and ale
- ⅛ teaspoon nutmeg
- ¼ teaspoon cinnamon
- ¼ teaspoon ground ginger
- *optional:* ¼ cup melted butter

Directions

1. Roast the apples in a baking pan at 450° for about an hour until they are very soft and begin to burst. (An alternative and quicker procedure is to peel and boil the apples until they are soft and flaky.) Leave apples whole or break them up.

2. In a large saucepan, dissolve the sugar, a few tablespoons at a time, in the cider, tasting for sweetness. Add the spices and melted butter.

3. Bring mixture to a boil and simmer for 10 to 15 minutes.

4. Pour the liquid over the apples in a large punch bowl, or serve in large, heat resistant mugs.

WORSHIP

Closing Prayer

Choose one of the following for your closing prayer optional activities:

If you have planned a Star Carol procession, you might make it the last activity of the Celebration. Singing Epiphany hymns, wind your way toward a crèche that rests somewhere in your church or home. Gather there, kneeling to pray.

If you made the Epiphany Star of felt, invite each group to tell what its symbol represents and to give thanks for the good news revealed in that symbol, for example:

> *Our wine jar stands for the miracle at Cana when Jesus turned water into wine. We give thanks to you, Lord, that your power works miracles of transformation, not only long ago, but in our lives today.*

If the group includes many children, you may want to darken the room where you are meeting and shine a flashlight on the ceiling. As you shine the light on each person, including yourself, pray, "Thank you, Jesus, that you are the light of the world. Thank you Jesus for your light that shines in each one of us. Show us how to share that light with others." Conclude by saying *Amen* together.